FATHERING STRONG

GOD'S BLUEPRINT FOR LEADING YOUR FAMILY

Real stories with Biblical wisdom to
guide your fatherhood journey

BRUCE STAPLETON

WestBow
PRESS®
A DIVISION OF THOMAS NELSON
& ZONDERVAN

WestBow Press books may be ordered through booksellers or by contacting:

WestBow Press
A Division of Thomas Nelson & Zondervan
1663 Liberty Drive
Bloomington, IN 47403
www.westbowpress.com
844-714-3454

ISBN: 979-8-3850-4684-3 (sc)
ISBN: 979-8-3850-4683-6 (e)

Print information available on the last page.

WestBow Press rev. date: 04/11/2025

CONTENTS

Dedication   vii

Acknowledgments   ix

Introduction: The Path to Fathering Strong   xi

**PART 1: THE FOUNDATION OF FATHERING STRONG -
BUILDING THE PILLARS OF A STRONG FATHER**   1

Chapter 1   The Call to Fathering Strong   3
Chapter 2   Building Your Armor - God as Protector, Order
                Keeper, Provider, and Stabilizer   7
Chapter 3   Courage - Facing the World Head-On   22
Chapter 4   Fortitude - The Unwavering Strength of a Father's
                Heart   31
Chapter 5   Faith - The Anchoring Strength of a Fathering
                Strong Life   37
Chapter 6   Love - The Heart of Fathering Strong   42

**PART 2: FROM FOUNDATION TO ACTION: BUILDING
YOUR FATHERING STRONG BLUEPRINT**   49

Chapter 7   Setting Your Course - How Goals Make You Stronger   51
Chapter 8   Physical Health - Fueling Your Body and Mind   57
Chapter 9   Spiritual Health - Connecting with the True Father   76
Chapter 10 Emotional Wealth - Mastering Your Inner World   97
Chapter 11 Financial Wisdom: Stewarding God's Resources
                as a Father   112
Chapter 12 A Strong Marriage: The Foundation of the Family   130
Chapter 13 Building Lasting Bonds with Your Children   145

PART 3: LIVING THE FATHERING STRONG LIFE   171

Chapter 14 Putting It All Together - Linking Goals to
              Fathering Strong   173
Chapter 15 Tools for Transformation - Building the Father
              You Want to Be   181
Chapter 16 The Power of the Fathering Strong Community   188
Chapter 17 Leaving a Legacy: The Impact of Fathering Strong   191

Epilogue – Fatherhood Stories   195
Appendix A - Fathering Strong Vision Worksheet   207
Appendix B - SMART Goal Blueprint Summary Worksheet   211
Appendix C - Fathering Strong Weekly Check-in Plan Worksheet   217
Appendix D - Daily Devotional and Journal Template   221
About the Author   225
Biblical Reference   227
Works Cited   231

DEDICATION

To my father, Samuel Baxter Stapleton, Jr., who taught me the meaning of strength through quiet wisdom and unwavering dedication. His steady presence in my life showed me that true fatherhood isn't measured in grand gestures, but in the countless small moments of love, guidance, and sacrifice. The way he lived his faith—not just in words, but in daily actions—set a foundation that I still build upon today.

And to my grandfather, Aubrey William Edwards, whose legacy of faith and family continues to echo through generations. His stories, prayers, and gentle spirit taught me that being a strong man means having a tender heart. He showed me how to balance firm conviction with deep compassion, and how to lead a family with both strength and grace.

Together, these two men demonstrated what it truly means to be Fathering Strong. Their examples shaped not only how I parent my own children but also how I understand God's heart as our heavenly Father. The seeds of faith, integrity, and perseverance they planted continue to bear fruit in our family tree.

May this book honor their legacy and help other fathers create the same kind of lasting impact they have had on me.

ACKNOWLEDGMENTS

This book emerged from my journey of learning and growing as a father. I couldn't have written it without the help and support of many remarkable people.

I want to extend my heartfelt gratitude to Pastor Eli Williams. Through his unwavering commitment to strengthening families and his decades of leadership in fatherhood programs, he has touched countless lives. As the founder and driving force behind Urban Light Ministries, he has created a powerful platform for positive change in our community, and I'm truly honored to collaborate with him on the Fathering Strong movement. His deep wisdom and extensive experience in supporting fathers have profoundly shaped this book's message and mission.

To my amazing wife, Priscilla, thank you. Your love and support have sustained me through all the ups and downs of being a father and now grandfather. You've been the bedrock for our four children, creating a stable and loving home where they could thrive. Your strength and belief in me have made everything possible. Not only have you been my partner in life and parenting, but you've also been my most trusted editor—both of this book and of my life itself. Your careful attention to every word I've written, coupled with your gentle but honest feedback, has made this book infinitely better. I will always be grateful for having you by my side.

To my four wonderful children, Michelle, Baxter, Alex, and Christine, thank you for all the fun times, challenges, and stories we've shared. Each of you, with your unique personality, has enriched my life and taught me countless lessons about being a father and, more importantly, a Godly man. You've inspired me to be a better person and dad, and I'm so proud of all of you.

To my sisters Carol Allen and Amy Stapleton, your unwavering support throughout the years has meant the world to me and my family. You've been there to celebrate our joys and help us through challenges, watching our children grow and sharing in all of life's precious moments. I'm especially grateful for Carol's dedication in spending countless hours reviewing early drafts of this book, and to both of you for offering your keen insights and thoughtful suggestions that helped shape these pages into something truly meaningful.

Lastly, I want to thank all the fathers who are working hard to be great dads and have shared their stories with me. I'm especially grateful to the brave fathers who contributed their personal experiences to this book— your willingness to open up about both your struggles and victories has been truly inspiring. Thank you for your honesty and vulnerability in sharing what it really means to be Fathering Strong. Your dedication to becoming better dads and your authentic stories have not only shaped this book but will undoubtedly encourage countless other fathers on their journey.

All of the stories in this book come from real experiences, either my own or those of other fathers. While most names have been changed to protect privacy, and some stories have been slightly modified to fit specific references and situations, the heart and truth of each story remain intact.

INTRODUCTION: THE PATH TO FATHERING STRONG

The first time I held my newborn daughter, her tiny fingers wrapped around mine, with a slight tilt of her head she looked right into my eyes. At that moment, I felt overwhelmed with happiness, wonder, and an immense sense of responsibility. I promised myself I would be the best father I could be - guiding her, protecting her, and helping her grow into a strong, confident woman. Nothing in my life had prepared me for the power of this moment. Like many new fathers, I stood there both excited and uncertain about the journey ahead.

Maybe you're feeling that same mix of joy and uncertainty right now. Or perhaps you've been a dad for years but still question if you're doing enough. Here's what I've learned: Fathering Strong isn't about being perfect - it's about setting clear, measurable goals and growing in faith through intentional action each day.

Think of this book as sitting down with a fellow dad who has walked this path before you. Through over 35 personal stories from my journey of raising four children and becoming a grandfather, along with 85 powerful stories from 20 different fathers, you'll find real-world wisdom that resonates with your own experience. More importantly, you'll discover how to lean on God's wisdom instead of just your own, with over 160 biblical references woven throughout to ground every principle in Scripture. Every story, lesson, and practical goal in these pages comes from real experience - both the victories and the mistakes.

You might be wondering, "What makes a strong father?" Our culture throws all kinds of expectations at dads. We're supposed to be providers, protectors, teachers, bankers, and role models. It can feel overwhelming. But God's word gives us a clearer picture and specific benchmarks to guide us. Just as our Father in heaven guides us with love, wisdom, and patience (James 1:5), He calls us to lead our families the same way.

This book is especially close to my heart because I know many of you grew up without a father figure. That absence can leave deep wounds and big questions about how to be the dad you never had. But here's the good news: through your relationship with God, you have access to the perfect Father. As it says in 2 Corinthians 6:18, "I will be a Father to you, and you will be my sons and daughters, says the Lord Almighty." By understanding His love and following His example, you can break negative cycles and create a new legacy of Fathering Strong for your family.

Here is what we'll achieve together:

> Setting specific spiritual and parenting goals that align with Scripture
> Learning measurable ways to demonstrate love and leadership daily
> Creating attainable action steps for building your faith while building your family
> Establishing relevant priorities that match God's plan for fathers
> Following time-bound strategies to put on God's armor for life's challenges

Each chapter combines three essential elements for Fathering Strong:

1. Real stories from my journey and other dads
2. Biblical wisdom that guides our goal-setting
3. SMART goals and action steps you can implement today

This isn't just about learning – it's about doing. James 1:22 reminds us to ".. not merely listen to the word, and so deceive yourselves. Do what it says." That's why you'll find clear, measurable action steps and prayer points throughout the book. These help you turn good intentions into daily habits that strengthen your fatherhood journey.

For years, I thought being a "strong" father meant having all the answers and never showing weakness. But God showed me something different. **Fathering Strong** comes from being real with our kids, admitting when we're wrong, and showing them how to depend on God's grace. When I started opening up about my struggles and pointing my children toward God's wisdom instead of just my own, our relationships grew stronger.

Remember this: God didn't call you to be a perfect father. He called you to be a faithful one who consistently works toward growth. Whether you're holding your first newborn or watching your children raise their own kids, it's never too late to start Fathering Strong through measurable goals and faithful action.

Ready to begin? Let's start this journey together, armed with God's Word and equipped with practical steps to strengthen your fatherhood journey.

PART 1

THE FOUNDATION OF FATHERING STRONG - BUILDING THE PILLARS OF A STRONG FATHER

Being a father is one of life's most important callings - a journey that fills each day with moments of joy, unexpected challenges and chances to grow in ways you never imagined. True fatherhood requires more than good intentions; it demands a rock-solid foundation built on timeless principles that can weather the complexities of raising children in today's world. In this first part, we'll explore what it truly means to be **"Fathering Strong"** - a concept that goes beyond basic parenting to embrace the divine purpose God has ordained for fathers. We'll discover how faith in God provides the wisdom, strength, and guidance essential for this holy responsibility while examining the core virtues that transforms men into the fathers they were created to be.

Our relationships with our fathers profoundly shape how we approach fatherhood ourselves. Some of us grew up without fathers and lack that foundational knowledge. Others had dads who were physically present but emotionally distant, or who modeled behaviors we actively choose not to repeat. Even those blessed with good father figures acknowledge their dads weren't perfect. These diverse experiences often leave us uncertain about our own journeys as fathers.

Yet there is profound hope in this truth: God, our perfect Father in heaven, provides the ultimate blueprint for fatherhood. Through His example, we see the perfect balance of protection and guidance, discipline and nurture, provision and presence. His model shows us that authentic fatherhood creates a sanctuary of safety, establishes loving boundaries, meets both physical and emotional needs, and offers unwavering stability. By embracing God's model of fatherhood, we can break free from any negative patterns from our past and forge new legacies of faithful fathering - regardless of our own upbringing.

At the heart of Fathering Strong lie four essential virtues: **courage, fortitude, faith, and love**. These aren't abstract concepts - they are the foundational pillars of God-centered fatherhood. Consider them your spiritual compass for navigating the challenges of modern parenting, building lasting connections with your children, and creating a legacy that glorifies both God and family.

Like a house built on bedrock that stands firm against storms, these four virtues provide the unshakeable foundation for strong fatherhood. They equip you with the strength, resilience, and steadfast purpose needed to face life's challenges while nurturing a family environment filled with love, joy, and eternal purpose.

In the chapters that follow, we'll examine each virtue in detail, exploring how they manifest in a father's daily walk and offering practical guidance for cultivating them. We'll begin by understanding God as our perfect Father, whose divine example illuminates the path to developing these crucial qualities.

These four virtues - courage, fortitude, faith, and love - work in perfect harmony to shape a father prepared for every season and challenge. As we explore each virtue, you'll discover practical ways to grow in these areas and embrace your calling as a Fathering Strong dad.

CHAPTER 1

THE CALL TO FATHERING STRONG

Tired. Frustrated. Confused.

I remember sitting in my car after a particularly rough day, my son's angry voice still ringing in my ears from our latest argument. These weren't just feelings anymore—they were my daily reality as I struggled to figure out how to be a good dad. The world bombarded me with contradicting advice: "Be their best friend!" some said. "No, be strict and demanding!" others argued. "Just throw money at the problem," whispered the guilt-ridden voice in my head. It was enough to leave any dad feeling lost.

But what if there was a better way? What if, instead of chasing every new parenting trend, we focused on what really matters: **raising strong, confident kids who can handle life's challenges?**

That's exactly what this book is about. It's not another manual of dos and don'ts—it's a blueprint to becoming the kind of dad who makes a real difference in his children's lives. A dad who is present, engaged, and a powerful force for good in his family.

Let me share some real stories I've witnessed:

- ›   Stephen, a single dad who spent years afraid to connect emotionally with his son after divorce, finally found the courage to open up. Now they share not just a home but their hopes, fears, and dreams.

- James, who used to spend 70-hour weeks at his software development firm, now dedicates Sunday afternoons to walks with his daughter Sarah. These walks have created a special space where she feels comfortable opening up about her life
- Carlos, who grew up with an angry father, broke the cycle by learning to breathe through his frustration and talk to his teenage son with patience and understanding.

These transformations aren't fairy tales—they're real examples of men who embraced the four pillars of being a strong father: courage, fortitude, faith, and love. Through this book, you'll discover practical ways to grow stronger in every aspect of your life—your physical health, spiritual health, emotional well-being, financial stability, and family relationships.

WHAT DOES IT MEAN TO BE "FATHERING STRONG"?

Let me be clear: Fathering Strong isn't about bench-pressing 250 pounds or having the biggest house on the block. It's about developing inner strength—the kind that shows up when your teenager is struggling, when your toddler has a meltdown, or when your family faces unexpected challenges. As Ephesians 6:4 reminds us, we are to "bring them up in the training and instruction of the Lord," while Psalm 103:13 beautifully illustrates that "as a father has compassion on his children, so the Lord has compassion on those who fear him." This inner strength is what Joshua 1:9 speaks of when God commands us to "be strong and courageous. Do not be afraid; do not be discouraged, for the Lord your God will be with you wherever you go."

The Apostle Paul captured this perfectly when he wrote:

"Be on your guard; stand firm in the faith; be courageous; be strong. Do everything in love." (1 Corinthians 16:13-14)

Steve Farrar, in his book *Point Man* (Farrar 2022), unpacks this beautifully. He explains that *"acting like men"* isn't about machismo—it's about courage and fortitude. It means having the strength to stand up for what's right, the willingness to take risks for your family, and an uncompromising faith in God. Most importantly, it means doing all of this with love as your foundation.

LIVING THE FOUR PILLARS

Think of these four pillars—courage, fortitude, faith, and love—as the legs of a table. When one is weak, everything on top becomes unstable. Let me break down what each means as a father in the real-world:

> - **Courage** - I once had to admit to my kids that I'd made a mistake in handling a family situation. My pride wanted to defend my actions, but courage meant saying, "I was wrong, and I'm sorry." That moment actually strengthened our relationship more than a thousand "perfect" parenting moments.
> - **Fortitude** - Remember Carlos from earlier? His fortitude showed when he stuck with anger management classes for six months straight, even when progress felt slow. Today, his teenage son comes to him for advice instead of avoiding him.
> - **Faith** - This isn't just about attending church—it's about living with purpose and teaching our kids that there's something bigger than ourselves. One dad I know starts each day reading a bible verse with his children over breakfast. Simple, consistent, powerful.
> - **Love** - This is what ties everything together. Every tough conversation, every disciplinary moment, every celebration needs to be grounded in love. It's what transforms our actions from mere parenting techniques into meaningful moments that shape our children's lives.

THE POWER OF A PRESENT FATHER

My own father taught me this through his actions more than his words. One memory stands out. I was twelve years old when I broke an expensive lamp playing ball in the house. Instead of exploding in anger (which I deserved), he took me into his workshop and showed me how to repair the lamp. That moment taught me about responsibility, problem-solving, and grace—all wrapped in love.

A CHALLENGE MANY FACE

Through the years, I've met countless men who never had a strong father figure to learn from. They're trying to write their own story without a blueprint, to play a role without ever seeing it performed well. If that's you, I want you to know something important: your past doesn't have to dictate your future as a father. You have the power to rewrite your family's story and break the cycle of absence and the fatherhood curse.

YOUR JOURNEY STARTS HERE

This book is your blueprint. In Part One, we'll dive deeper into each of these four pillars of what it means to be Fathering Strong, exploring practical ways to build them into your daily life. In Part Two, we'll tackle the six key strengths you need to maximize your health, wealth, and relationships and how to set goals for lasting change.

Think back to that scene I described at the beginning of this chapter—sitting alone in my car, overwhelmed by the weight of fatherhood, wrestling with my son's angry words and my own inadequacy. Perhaps you've experienced a similar moment of doubt and frustration. But here's what I've learned: those moments of crisis often become turning points. They're opportunities to choose a different path, to embrace a stronger way of fathering. Whether you're reading this during a sleepless night or stealing a few quiet moments during your workday, know that this journey toward Fathering Strong transforms not just how you parent but who you are as a man.

This isn't just about becoming a better dad. It's about becoming the man God designed you to be—strong in character, purpose, and love. Let's take this first step together. Your children are worth it, and so are you.

CHAPTER 2

BUILDING YOUR ARMOR - GOD AS PROTECTOR, ORDER KEEPER, PROVIDER, AND STABILIZER

I'll never forget the night my daughter smashed her finger in the door during my son's Cub Scout pinewood derby event. She was only five years old, and her screams pierced through the crowded room. My heart pounding, I scooped her up and rushed her to urgent care, terrified her finger might be broken. In that moment of complete powerlessness, watching my little girl in pain, I understood Paul's words about the "The Armor of God" (Shirer 2015) in a profound new way. Sometimes, being a father means facing unexpected battles - moments when we desperately need divine protection, not just for ourselves but for the precious ones we'd give anything to shield from harm.

In Ephesians 6:10-18, Paul describes this spiritual armor in detail - the belt of truth, the breastplate of righteousness, feet fitted with the gospel of peace, the shield of faith, the helmet of salvation, and the sword of the Spirit. Each piece serves a vital purpose in our spiritual battles. Just as a soldier wouldn't dream of entering combat without proper protection, we fathers need this divine armor to guard our hearts and minds as we lead our families. When my daughter was hurt that night, I realized that while I couldn't prevent every physical injury, I could arm myself with God's strength to guide her through life's challenges with wisdom and grace.

For many of you—especially those who grew up without a father figure—understanding God's role as our heavenly Father is life-changing. Mike, a father in one of our Fathering Strong communities, once shared how growing up with an absent dad left him feeling lost about how to parent his own children. "I had no blueprint". But when I started seeing God as my Father, everything changed. He became my model, my guide."

Before we explore how to become better fathers through courage, fortitude, faith, and love, we must first understand how God fathers us. He's not some distant figure in the sky—He's intimately involved in our daily lives as our divine protector, order keeper, provider, and stabilizer. Understanding these aspects of God's character isn't just about healing from our past; it's about learning to embody these qualities in our own parenting journey.

Let me be real with you: this isn't just about reading words on a page. It's about allowing God's truth to transform how you think, act, and love your kids in real, everyday moments.

GOD AS PROTECTOR

Tom, a single dad, once told me how he used to lie awake at night, worried sick about his teenage daughter's safety. "I can't be everywhere," he'd say. That's when Psalm 91:4 became his lifeline: "He will cover you with His feathers, and under His wings, you will find refuge." Tom started praying this verse over his daughter every night, and something beautiful happened—his anxiety began to lift as he learned to trust God's protection.

I remember when my own daughter started driving. That first night she took the car alone, I paced our living room like a caged lion. My wife finally sat me down and reminded me of something crucial: our job isn't to be all-powerful protectors—that's God's role. Our job is to teach our children to recognize and trust in God's protection.

Let me share another story that really drove this home. A few years ago, John, a father who helped with our junior swim team, faced every parent's nightmare when his son was diagnosed with cancer. During one particularly difficult night in the hospital, John felt completely helpless. "I couldn't fight the cancer for him," he told us later. "I couldn't guarantee everything would be okay. But I could show him how to trust in God's protection, even in the scariest moments."

John started a ritual with his son. Every morning during treatment, they would read a Bible verse about God's protection together. They called it their *"shield of faith"* time, inspired by Ephesians 6:16. The nurses noticed how this simple practice changed both father and son—bringing peace in the midst of uncertainty.

Trusting in God's protection doesn't mean we become passive about our children's safety. Instead, it gives us the wisdom and confidence to make sound decisions without being paralyzed by fear. Think of it like teaching a child to swim. We don't just throw them in the deep end and say "God will protect you!" We stay close, we teach them proper techniques, we use flotation devices when needed—but ultimately, we know that God's protection goes far beyond what our human efforts can provide.

The Bible gives us powerful images of God's protection that we can share with our children. Let me break these down into practical, everyday applications.

God as our Shield and Fortress

When my son was terrified of thunderstorms, we turned Psalm 18:30 into a bedroom poster: "As for God—his way is perfect; the Lord's word is flawless; he shields all who take refuge in him." Now, every crash of thunder becomes a reminder of God's protection rather than a source of fear.

God as our Guard and Watchman

During a family camping trip, we used the night sky to teach our kids about Psalm 121:7-8: "The Lord will keep you from all harm—he will watch over your life; the Lord will watch over your coming and going both now and forevermore." Just as the stars keep their watch through the night, God never sleeps on His job of protecting us.

God as our Deliverer and Rescuer

When my daughter faced bullying in middle school, we found strength in Isaiah 41:10: "So do not fear, for I am with you; do not be dismayed, for I am your God. I will strengthen you and help you; I will uphold you with my righteous right hand." This verse became her daily ammunition against fear. She eventually used this strength to create a program on the effects of bullying, where she received a Girl Scout Gold Award.

God as our Hiding Place

After losing their home to a fire, Mark's family discovered a new meaning in Psalm 32:7: "You are my hiding place; you will protect me from trouble and surround me with songs of deliverance." They learned that true security isn't in walls and roofs, but in God's faithful presence.

Remember, our role isn't to be perfect protectors—that's an impossible standard that will crush us. Instead, we're called to be living examples of what it means to trust in God's perfect protection. When our children see us actively relying on God's protection in our own lives, they learn to do the same.

As you face your own challenges in protecting your family, remember Tom's transformation from anxious nights to peaceful trust. Let's teach our children that while we can't always be there to protect them, they have a heavenly Father whose protection never fails. This isn't just about keeping them physically safe—it's about nurturing a deep, lasting faith that will sustain them long after they leave our homes.

GOD AS ORDER KEEPER

"My house was chaos," laughed Carlos, a father of four who is part of a Dad's group on Fathering Strong. The kids were staying up until midnight, meals were random, and homework was always a last-minute panic." Their story probably sounds familiar to many of us. Carlos admitted feeling overwhelmed until one of the dads in the group suggested looking at how God brings order to chaos.

Let's start where God Starts – in the beginning.

Genesis 1 shows us something remarkable about God's nature as an order keeper. He didn't create everything at once in a big bang of creativity. Instead, He worked methodically:

> Day 1: He separated light from darkness, creating day and night
> Day 2: He created the sky and separated the waters above from the waters below
> Day 3: He gathered the waters and created dry land, then made vegetation
> Day 4: He created the sun, moon, and stars to mark seasons and time
> Day 5: He filled the seas with fish and the skies with birds
> Day 6: He created land animals and humans
> Day 7: He rested, establishing the pattern of rest

This wasn't because God needed six days—it was to show us the importance of ordered processes. As David, a father of two teenagers, told me, "When I studied creation, I realized God's not into chaos. He's into step-by-step transformation."

Here's how this played out in David's family. Like many of us, his mornings were pure mayhem—kids missing buses, forgotten homework, skipped breakfasts. Taking a cue from Genesis, he created what he calls *"First Things First"*:

1. Wake-up routine (alarms set the night before)
2. Personal care (hygiene, getting dressed)
3. Spiritual nourishment (brief family devotional)
4. Physical nourishment (breakfast together)
5. Day preparation (backpacks, sports gear, etc.)

"It's not just about getting things done," David explains. "It's about teaching our kids that order reflects God's character."

The Bible gives us numerous examples of God's order-keeping nature:

God's Order in Creation

- Jeremiah 33:25-26 reminds us that God established the laws of heaven and earth
- Psalm 104:19 tells us, "He made the moon to mark the seasons, and the sun knows when to go down"
- Job 38:33 asks, "Do you know the laws of the heavens? Can you set up God's dominion over the earth?"

God's Order in Leadership

- In Exodus 18:17-23, we see God's wisdom through Jethro, teaching Moses to establish ordered leadership
- 1 Corinthians 14:33 declares, "For God is not a God of disorder but of peace"
- Titus 1:5 shows Paul's instruction to "put in order what was left unfinished"

James, a father struggling with work-life balance, used these principles to restructure his family leadership. "I was trying to handle everything myself, just like Moses," he admits. "Now I've learned to delegate age-appropriate responsibilities to each child, creating order through shared leadership."

God's Order in Worship and Life

- Leviticus provides detailed instructions for ordered worship
- 1 Chronicles 23:28-32 shows David organizing temple service
- Colossians 2:5 praises "how disciplined you are and how firm your faith in Christ is"

The beautiful thing about God's order is that it's not rigid or oppressive. As Psalm 19:7-9 tells us, "The law of the Lord is perfect, refreshing the soul." When we establish godly order in our homes, we're not creating a prison of rules—we're building a framework for freedom and growth.

Remember, establishing order is a process. Start small. Maybe begin with regular meal times or a consistent bedtime routine. As Proverbs 3:6 promises, "In all your ways submit to him, and he will make your paths straight."

The goal isn't perfection—it's progress. As we model God's order-keeping nature in our homes, we're teaching our children something profound about His character and His love for us. We're showing them that in a world that often feels chaotic, they can always find peace in God's perfect order.

GOD AS PROVIDER

The day I had to close my state-of-the-art fitness center—which had created the Lifegevity program that will be referenced in future chapters—still stands vivid in my memory. After investing thousands of dollars in facility improvements, I learned that another company had purchased our building. The new owners had other plans for the space, and I simply couldn't afford to relocate the business. With four kids, a mortgage, and only one month of savings, I felt like I was drowning. That's when my wife shared something that changed my perspective: "God's provision doesn't always look like what we expect. Go to the church chapel, get on your knees, and ask God for guidance and wisdom."

Let me tell you about Matthew 6:26, a verse that became my lifeline during that time: "Look at the birds of the air; they do not sow or reap or store away in barns, and yet your heavenly Father feeds them. Are you not much more valuable than they?" Every morning, I'd watch the birds outside my window while drinking coffee, reminding myself of this truth.

GOD'S PROVISION IN UNEXPECTED WAYS

Let me continue with my story. After I had to close my business, I had many sleepless nights about how I was going to provide for my four children. College expenses were close, the mortgage needed to be paid, and I had no job. I kept praying for God to show me some sign that things would get better. The next day, I found a job ad in the paper that I applied for and was called for an interview. My oldest daughter, who worked part-time, announced that she would purchase the Christmas tree that year since she knew how much that would help. We received an anonymous gift card to Kroger in our mailbox to help with food expenses.

This mirrors the biblical story of Elijah in 1 Kings 17:2-6, where God used ravens to bring bread and meat to the prophet: "The ravens brought him bread and meat in the morning and bread and meat in the evening, and he drank from the brook." Sometimes God's provision comes through unexpected channels.

TEACHING OUR CHILDREN ABOUT GOD'S PROVISION

Here's how some fathers in our community teach their children about God's provision:

> - **The Blessing Jar** - Steve's family keeps what they call a "Blessing Jar," inspired by Malachi 3:10: "Test me in this," says the LORD Almighty, "and see if I will not throw open the floodgates of heaven and pour out so much blessing that there will not be room enough to store it." They write down every instance of God's provision, big or small, and read them during family devotions.
> - **The First Fruits Principle** - Mike teaches his children about giving from Proverbs 3:9-10: "Honor the LORD with your wealth, with the first fruits of all your crops; then your barns will be filled to overflowing." Even when money is tight, his

family sets aside the first portion for God, teaching his children to trust in divine provision.

> **The Daily Bread Exercise** - Inspired by Matthew 6:11 ("Give us today our daily bread"), John's family practices gratitude at every meal, specifically naming how God provided that food—from the farmers who grew it to the paycheck that purchased it.

BIBLICAL PROMISES OF PROVISION

Let's explore some key promises about God's provision that can transform how we view our role as providers:

Complete Provision

> Philippians 4:19: "And my God will meet all your needs according to the riches of his glory in Christ Jesus."

> Psalm 34:10: "The lions may grow weak and hungry; but those who seek the LORD lack no good thing."

Wisdom in Provision

> James 1:5: "If any of you lacks wisdom, you should ask God, who gives generously to all without finding fault, and it will be given to you."

> Proverbs 2:6-7: "For the LORD gives wisdom; from his mouth come knowledge and understanding. He holds success in store for the upright, he is a shield to those whose walk is blameless."

Spiritual Provision

> 2 Peter 1:3: "His divine power has given us everything we need for a godly life through our knowledge of him who called us by his own glory and goodness."

> Ephesians 1:3 "Praise be to the God and Father of our Lord Jesus Christ, who has blessed us in the heavenly realms with every spiritual blessing in Christ."

A FATHER'S PRAYER FOR PROVISION

Let me share a prayer that has helped many fathers.

"Lord, help me trust You as my ultimate provider. When I'm tempted to worry about providing for my family, remind me of Your faithfulness. Help me teach my children that every good gift comes from You (James 1:17). Give me wisdom to manage the resources You've entrusted to me, and show me how to model generosity even in times of scarcity. Amen."

Remember, fathers, our role as providers isn't about carrying the whole burden alone—it's about partnering with God and teaching our children to trust in His provision. As Psalm 127:1 reminds us, "Unless the LORD builds the house, the builders labor in vain."

GOD AS STABILIZER

Let me tell you about David, a father who lost his wife to cancer. During one of our meetings, he shared something profound: "I used to think being stable meant never showing weakness to my kids. Now I realize it means showing them how to lean on God when you're breaking inside."

BIBLICAL FOUNDATIONS OF GOD'S STABILITY

Throughout scripture, we see God repeatedly described as our rock, fortress, and anchor:

- ▸ Psalm 62:2: "Truly he is my rock and my salvation; he is my fortress, I will never be shaken."
- ▸ 2 Samuel 22:47: "The Lord lives! Praise be to my Rock! Exalted be my God, the Rock, my Savior!"
- ▸ Deuteronomy 32:4: "He is the Rock, his works are perfect, and all his ways are just."

These aren't just poetic metaphors—they're promises we can build our lives upon.

GOD'S STABILITY IN ACTION

Consider these powerful biblical examples.

- ➤ Daniel's Unwavering Faith
  - Despite life-threatening pressure to conform, Daniel maintained his prayer routine three times daily (Daniel 6:10)
  - The result? Even his enemies acknowledged the stability of his faith (Daniel 6:26-27)
- ➤ Paul's Secret of Contentment
  - "I have learned to be content whatever the circumstances" (Philippians 4:11-13)
  - His stability came from knowing Christ was his strength
- ➤ David's Anchor in Chaos
  - While running from Saul, David wrote, "When I am afraid, I put my trust in you" (Psalm 56:3)
  - Even in exile, he maintained emotional stability through trust in God

Think about Jesus's parable in Matthew 7:24-27 about the wise man who built his house on rock versus the foolish man who built on sand. When storms came—and they always do—only the house with the proper foundation remained standing. This isn't just about construction; it's about building our families on the unchanging nature of God.

As James 1:17 reminds us, God is the Father "who does not change like shifting shadows." A local pastor who works in our church counseling ministry shares this verse with every struggling family: "Jesus Christ is the same yesterday and today and forever" (Hebrews 13:8). In a world where everything seems to shift like desert sands, God remains our constant.

A FATHER'S PRAYER FOR STABILITY

Here's a prayer you can use when you feel your life is in chaos and you need stability:

"Heavenly Father, when life feels uncertain and I struggle to provide stability for my family, remind me that You are my rock and fortress (Psalm 18:2). Help me model trust in Your unchanging nature. Give me wisdom to create stable environments that honor You, and faith to lead my family through life's storms. In Jesus' name, Amen."

Remember, true stability isn't about having everything under control—it's about being under God's control. As Isaiah 26:4 promises, "Trust in the LORD forever, for the LORD, the LORD himself, is the Rock eternal."

By anchoring our families in God's unchanging character, we provide them with something far more valuable than temporal stability—we give them an unshakeable foundation for life. As Solomon wrote in Proverbs 10:25, "When the storm has swept by, the wicked are gone, but the righteous stand firm forever."

THE ARMOR OF GOD: YOUR FOUNDATION FOR FATHERHOOD

About a year ago, we did a poll on Fathering Strong where we asked what are your biggest parenting fears. The answers were eye-opening: *"That I'll mess up my kids like my dad messed me up." "That I won't be able to protect them from what's out there." "That they'll walk away from their faith."*

These honest admissions remind us why Paul's metaphor of the Armor of God in Ephesians 6:10-18 is so relevant for fathers today. This isn't just ancient military imagery—it's a blueprint for spiritual fatherhood that perfectly aligns with our four core virtues of Fathering Strong.

THE SHIELD: OUR CENTRAL SYMBOL

You might have noticed that Fathering Strong and the cover of this book use a shield as its design and logo. This isn't just about protection—it represents the shield of faith described in Ephesians 6:16: "In addition to all this, take up the shield of faith, with which you can extinguish all the flaming arrows of the evil one."

The Roman shield (scutum) Paul referenced wasn't just a defensive tool. It was also used to advance forward in formation with other soldiers. This perfectly captures our vision of fathers moving forward together, protecting their families while advancing God's kingdom. Like these shields that could link together, we are stronger when we stand together as fathers.

CONNECTING THE ARMOR TO FOUR VIRTUES OF FATHERING STRONG

Here's where it gets practical. Each piece of the armor Paul describes lines up perfectly with the core virtues we emphasize at Fathering Strong. When we understand how these ancient pieces of armor connect to our modern-day challenges as dads, we discover a powerful framework for protecting and guiding our families. Let's break down how each virtue pairs with specific pieces of armor.

- > **Courage:** The Breastplate of Righteousness and Belt of Truth
  - Biblical Foundation: "Stand firm then, with the belt of truth buckled around your waist, with the breastplate of righteousness in place" (Ephesians 6:14)
  - Modern Application: Mike, a father of teens, shares: "When my daughter asked tough questions about faith, I needed the courage to admit when I didn't have all the answers. The belt of truth reminded me that authenticity matters more than appearing perfect."
- > **Fortitude:** The Feet Fitted with Readiness
  - Biblical Foundation: "and with your feet fitted with the readiness that comes from the gospel of peace" (Ephesians 6:15)

- Modern Application: James found this vital during his son's mental health crisis: "Standing firm meant being ready for lengthy battles. Some days, fortitude was simply showing up consistently with God's peace."
- **Faith:** The Shield of Faith and Helmet of Salvation
  - Biblical Foundation: "Take up the shield of faith...Take the helmet of salvation" (Ephesians 6:16-17)
  - Modern Application: Mark's family created a "Shield Wall" in their home—a prayer wall where they post challenges they're facing together in faith.
- **Love:** The Sword of the Spirit
  - Biblical Foundation: "And the sword of the Spirit, which is the word of God" (Ephesians 6:17)
  - Modern Application: Dr. Roberts teaches fathers: "The sword isn't just for battle—it's for surgery, carefully shaping our children's hearts with God's truth spoken in love."

THE POWER OF STANDING TOGETHER

Remember, no Roman soldier ever fought alone. Their strength came from standing shoulder to shoulder, shields overlapping. This is why our logo shows a shield—it represents both protection and unity. When fathers stand together, linking our shields of faith:

- We strengthen each other
- We protect more than just our families
- We advance God's kingdom together
- We create a legacy of faithful fatherhood

As we close this chapter, remember that putting on God's armor isn't a one-time event—it's a daily commitment to stand firm in faith, linked together with other fathers, advancing God's kingdom one family at a time. Through courage, we face the daily challenges of fatherhood head-on, making tough decisions and having difficult conversations. With fortitude, we persist through trials and setbacks, showing our children the power of resilience. Our faith becomes the foundation that sustains us and guides our families through life's storms. And love—the greatest of all virtues—transforms our actions from mere duty into sacred purpose, helping us raise children who know they are cherished by both their earthly and heavenly fathers. In the chapters ahead, we'll explore each virtue in detail but always remember: our strength comes not from the armor itself but from the God who provides it.

"Finally, be strong in the Lord and in his mighty power." (Ephesians 6:10)

CHAPTER 3

COURAGE - FACING THE
WORLD HEAD-ON

I'll never forget the morning I watched my five-year-old son step onto the school bus for the first time. As he climbed those giant steps, my heart raced faster than his. Would he make friends? Would he feel scared or alone? At that moment, I realized that fatherhood demands courage from us as parents, watching our children face life's challenges while we learn to let them grow.

A father needs courage to be the best dad possible, perhaps more than any other virtue. While faith gives us direction, fortitude provides endurance, and love fuels our purpose, it's courage that enables us to act on these noble qualities when fatherhood tests us. As Solomon writes in Proverbs 24:16, "For though the righteous fall seven times, they rise again." This resilience, this courage to keep rising, defines the journey of fatherhood.

Every day throws us into a world of uncertainty, where we face tough choices and must constantly grow and adapt. We're challenged to push beyond our comfort zones and confront our deepest fears - whether we're making difficult decisions about our children's future or acknowledging our own parental shortcomings.

But here's the thing - courage isn't about being fearless. **It's about taking action despite our fears,** driven by love for our kids and dedication to our families. This foundational virtue transforms our other strengths - faith, fortitude, and love - from mere ideals into active forces that shape our children's lives and leave lasting impressions on their hearts.

WAYS FATHERS NEED COURAGE

Earlier this year, I sat across from Mark, a fellow dad in a Men's Group, as he shared his struggle with setting boundaries for his teenage daughter's social media use. "I know she'll be angry," he confessed, "but I have to protect her, even if it makes me the bad guy." His story reminds us of the courage that fathers need every day.

To be a protector: When James discovered his son was being cyberbullied, he didn't just comfort his child - he took action. He documented everything, met with school administrators, and worked tirelessly to create a safer online environment for all students. "I was terrified of making things worse," he admitted, "but doing nothing wasn't an option." Sometimes protection means physical safety, but more often, it's about emotional security - having difficult conversations about peer pressure, online safety, or standing up against bullying.

To set boundaries: Mike, a father of three, shared how his daughter's tearful pleading for a later curfew almost broke his resolve. "Every fiber of my being wanted to give in," he told me. "But I knew midnight was too late for a fifteen-year-old, no matter how many of her friends were allowed to stay out." He stood firm, weathered the storm of teenage anger, and months later, his daughter thanked him for caring enough to say no. Setting limits isn't about being the "bad guy" - it's about having the courage to choose what's right over what's easy.

To admit mistakes: I'll never forget the day I lost my temper with my son over a spilled drink at dinner. The words came out harsh and cutting, and I immediately saw the hurt in his eyes. It took every ounce of courage to pull him aside later, look him in the eye, and say, "Daddy was wrong. I'm sorry for yelling, and I'm working on being more patient." That moment of vulnerability strengthened our relationship more than a thousand perfect parenting moments could have.

To face the unknown: Consider Phil, whose company offered him a promotion that would mean moving his family across the country. His kids were thriving in their current school, and his wife had a job she loved. "I was paralyzed with fear about making the wrong choice," he shared. "But I knew I had to gather information, pray about it, and make a decision - even without knowing exactly how it would turn out." Whether it's career changes, health challenges, or watching our children take risks, fatherhood constantly asks us to step into uncertainty with faith and courage.

To be a role model: Robert, an emergency room nurse, often works holiday shifts while his kids celebrate with their mom and extended family. "It breaks my heart to miss these moments," he shared, "but I want my children to see that serving others sometimes means personal sacrifice." Through his example, his kids are learning about integrity, responsibility, and putting values into action - even when it's difficult.

To show love and vulnerability: When John's teenage son was struggling with depression, he faced a choice: maintain the stoic facade he'd learned from his own father or open up about his own battles with mental health during college. "Sharing my story felt like jumping off a cliff," John recalled, "but watching my son's relief when he realized he wasn't alone - that was worth every second of discomfort." His courage to be vulnerable created a safe space for his son to seek help and begin healing.

These stories from real fathers show us that courage comes in many forms. Sometimes it roars like a lion when we're defending our children; other times, it whispers in quiet moments of vulnerability and truth. But always, it's driven by love - love that compels us to act despite our fears, to stand firm when it would be easier to give in, and to open our hearts when we're tempted to close them.

What I have learned over the years is that the most courageous thing a father can do is show up - day after day, decision after decision, choosing to be present and engaged even when it's uncomfortable or uncertain. This steady presence and unwavering courage become the bedrock upon which our children build their sense of security and their understsanding of what it means to face life's challenges with faith and determination.

STORIES OF EVERYDAY COURAGE - THE FATHER WHO NEVER GAVE UP

When David's son Noah was diagnosed with autism at age three, their world turned upside down. I watched my friend transform from an uncertain, overwhelmed father into a fierce advocate for his child. David's journey wasn't just about facing one big challenge - it was about finding courage every single day in ways most people never see.

"The first six months after the diagnosis, I felt like I was drowning," David confided during one of our weekly coffee meetings. "Every milestone Noah missed felt like a punch to the gut. While other parents were posting videos of their kids singing the alphabet, I was celebrating Noah finally making eye contact with me."

But David refused to let fear or uncertainty dictate his son's future. He spent countless nights researching autism therapies after Noah was asleep. He took a second job to afford specialized treatments that insurance wouldn't cover. When the local school district claimed they couldn't accommodate Noah's needs, David didn't just accept their answer - he educated himself about special education law and Noah's rights.

"Each meeting with the school board felt like climbing a mountain," he told me, "but Noah's smile kept me going. I realized that if I didn't fight for him, who would?"

The courage it took wasn't just in the big moments - the IEP meetings, the appeals, the difficult decisions about treatments. It showed up in small ways too, like when David started taking Noah to the park despite the stares from other parents who didn't understand his son's behaviors.

Or when he learned to sit calmly through his son's meltdowns in grocery stores, choosing to be present with Noah's struggles rather than feeling embarrassed by others' judgments.

"The hardest part," David shared, "was letting go of the future I'd imagined for Noah and finding the courage to embrace the beautiful, unexpected journey we're actually on. Some days that takes more courage than any meeting or therapy session."

One particular moment stands out in David's journey. After months of intensive speech therapy, Noah, then five, finally said "Dad" for the first time. It wasn't during a therapy session or a planned activity - it was during their nightly routine of looking at pictures of animals together. "In that moment," David said, his eyes welling up, "every late night, every extra shift, every uncomfortable conversation with teachers - it all felt worth it. But more than that, it reminded me why we never give up."

Today, Noah is twelve. He still faces challenges, but he's thriving in his own way. David's advocacy helped create an inclusive support program at their school that now helps other children with special needs. He leads a support group for other parents, sharing not just resources and advice but the kind of courage that comes from walking this path.

"The diagnosis felt like the end of the world," David reflected recently. "But it was really just the beginning of discovering what real courage means - showing up every day, fighting the battles no one sees, and choosing hope even when it feels impossible."

David's story reminds us that fatherly courage often looks different than we expect. It's not always about grand gestures or heroic moments. Sometimes, it's about the quiet determination to keep going, to keep learning, to keep advocating - even when progress comes in the smallest of steps. It's about finding strength not in spite of our fears and uncertainties but through them, transformed by love for our children.

As David often tells new parents in his support group, "Courage isn't about having all the answers. It's about being willing to look for them, even when the search feels overwhelming. And sometimes, the bravest thing we can do is simply show up for another day, ready to love our children exactly as they are."

BIBLICAL WISDOM FOR MODERN COURAGE

The Bible offers us powerful examples of fatherly courage that speak directly to our modern challenges. These aren't just ancient stories - they're mirrors reflecting our own daily struggles and victories as fathers.

Abraham: Courage to Trust God's Plan

Consider Abraham, whom we often call the father of faith. When God promised him a son in his old age, he wrestled with the same doubts many of us faced when life veered from our expected path. I remember sitting with my colleague Eric shortly after he was laid off from our company. His voice cracked as he asked, "How do I tell my kids everything will be okay when I'm not sure myself?" Abraham's story offered us both a powerful reminder: courage often means trusting God's promises even when the path ahead seems foggy.

Like Abraham, who "believed, and it was credited to him as righteousness" (Romans 4:3), Eric found strength in having an honest conversation with his children about their situation while holding onto hope. "We talked about Abraham waiting for Isaac," Eric later shared with me. "It helped my kids understand that sometimes God's best gifts require patient trust."

Joseph: Courage to Embrace Unexpected Fatherhood

Joseph's story particularly resonates with modern fathers who are raising children in complex family situations. He chose to father a child who wasn't biologically his, faced public scrutiny, and adapted his entire life to protect and provide for Jesus and Mary.

Fred, a stepfather to three teenagers, often draws strength from Joseph's example. "When I first married their mom, I felt like an outsider trying to find my place," he admitted. "But Joseph reminds me that being a father is about choosing to love and lead, regardless of circumstances."

Joshua: Courage to Stand for Faith in a Changing World

Joshua's command from God, "Be strong and courageous. Do not be afraid; do not be discouraged, for the Lord your God will be with you wherever you go" (Joshua 1:9), speaks powerfully to fathers raising children in today's challenging world. James, a father of two teenagers, recently shared how this verse gave him strength when making difficult parenting decisions about technology and social media.

"Knowing that God is with us gives me the courage to make tough choices," James explained. "It's not about following the crowd, but about leading our children with godly wisdom and conviction."

Remember, these biblical fathers weren't perfect - they were real men who faced real challenges with God's help. Their stories remind us that courage isn't about feeling fearless; it's about moving forward in faith, knowing that the same God who guided them guides us today in our journey of fatherhood.

As Solomon wisely noted, "The fear of the Lord is the beginning of wisdom" (Proverbs 9:10). When we ground our courage in faith, we find the strength not just to face our daily challenges but to lead our families toward God's promises with hope and confidence.

COURAGE GROWS THROUGH PRACTICE

In my thirty-plus years of fatherhood, I've learned that courage grows through practice. Each time we choose to face our fears - whether it's having a difficult conversation with our teenager, admitting we were wrong, or making an unpopular but necessary decision - we build our capacity for courage. And in doing so, we don't just become better fathers; we show our children what it means to live with faith, fortitude, and love in action.

As we close this chapter, remember that your journey as a father isn't about being fearless - it's about choosing to act with love even when fear is present. Your courage, combined with faith, fortitude, and love, creates a legacy that will echo through generations.

Take a moment today to recognize the courage you've already shown as a father, and ask God for the strength to face tomorrow's challenges with renewed bravery. Your children are watching, learning, and growing through your example of courageous love.

REFLECTIVE QUESTIONS ON HAVING COURAGE

1. When was the last time you showed courage in your parenting, and how did your children respond?
2. What specific fears or anxieties are currently holding you back from being the father you aspire to be?
3. In what ways can you intentionally demonstrate courage to your family this week?
4. Think of a time when you had to make an unpopular parenting decision - how did that experience shape your understanding of courage?
5. How do you balance protecting your children with allowing them to develop their own courage?
6. What role does your faith play in finding courage during difficult parenting moments?
7. Which biblical father's story resonates most with your current challenges, and why?
8. How can you nurture courage in each of your children's unique personalities?
9. What legacy of courage do you hope to leave for your children and grandchildren?

10. In what areas of fatherhood do you need to pray for more courage?

Remember, as Paul writes in 2 Timothy 1:7, *"For the Spirit of God gave us does not makes us timid, but gives us power, love and self-discipline."* This reminds us that courage isn't just about our own strength - it's about trusting in something greater than ourselves.

CHAPTER 4

FORTITUDE - THE UNWAVERING STRENGTH OF A FATHER'S HEART

I'll never forget the night we finally got answers about my son's constant ear infections. The pediatrician's office had become our second home – monthly visits, sleepless nights of him crying in pain, and countless rounds of antibiotics that seemed to offer only temporary relief. When the ENT specialist explained that my son would need tubes in his ears, I felt a mix of relief and anxiety. My world shifted as the doctor detailed the procedure for my four-year-old boy, who sat in my lap clutching his favorite stuffed animal. That day taught me what true fortitude means: it isn't about being fearless; it's about moving forward despite your fears.

Fatherhood isn't a sprint; it's a marathon. It's a journey filled with moments that test our resolve – from 3 AM feedings to teenage rebellions – demanding resilience, patience, and an unwavering commitment to our families. In this chapter, we'll explore fortitude, that inner strength that helps fathers persevere through adversity and emerge stronger, not just for ourselves but for those who depend on us.

THE OAK AND THE STORM

My neighbor Tom, a single father of three, lost his job during the pandemic. Instead of crumbling under the pressure, he transformed his garage into a workspace and started a small business building custom furniture. "Some days, I wanted to give up," he told me, "but when I saw my kids watching how I handled this setback, I knew I had to stay strong." Like a mighty oak standing tall against a fierce storm, Tom bent but didn't break. His story reminds us that fortitude isn't just about surviving the storm – it's about growing stronger through it.

This resilience in the face of adversity is something I've witnessed time and again in the fathers around me. Take David, a colleague whose wife was diagnosed with breast cancer. While maintaining his full-time job, he took on all the household responsibilities and still found time to help his kids with their homework every evening. "You just find the strength you didn't know you had," he shared during one of our lunch breaks. "It's like discovering muscles you never knew existed until you're forced to use them."

Then there's Carlos, who immigrated here twenty-five years ago with nothing but hope and determination. He worked three jobs while learning English at night, all to ensure his daughters could have the education he never received. Today, his eldest is heading to medical school. "The exhaustion was real," he told me with tears in his eyes at her graduation, "but seeing her in that cap and gown made every sleepless night worth it."

These stories share a common thread: ordinary men discovering extraordinary strength within themselves when circumstances demanded it. Like saplings that develop deeper roots in response to strong winds, these fathers grew stronger through their struggles. They demonstrate that fortitude isn't a trait we're born with – it's one we develop through facing and overcoming challenges, one day at a time.

BIBLICAL WISDOM FOR MODERN FORTITUDE

The Bible offers timeless guidance for fathers seeking strength in challenging times. Consider Joshua 1:9: "Be strong and courageous. Do not be afraid; do not be discouraged, for the Lord your God will be with you wherever you go." This verse speaks directly to fathers facing uncertain circumstances, reminding us that true fortitude comes from knowing we're not alone in our struggles.

King David's journey as both a leader and father provides powerful lessons in resilience. Despite his mistakes and hardships, he maintained his faith and eventually found redemption. His psalms, particularly Psalm 34:19 – "The righteous person may have many troubles, but the Lord delivers him from them all" – offer comfort to modern fathers facing their own trials.

The story of Job teaches us about maintaining integrity and faith through unimaginable hardship. His example reminds fathers that even when everything seems lost, holding onto our principles and trust in God can carry us through the darkest valleys. As Job declared, "Though he slay me, yet will I hope in him" (Job 13:15).

These ancient words of wisdom continue to resonate with fathers today, providing a foundation of strength that transcends time and circumstance. They remind us that fortitude isn't just about physical or emotional strength – it's also about spiritual endurance and faith in something greater than ourselves.

WHEN FAITH MEETS ACTION: A FATHER'S JOURNEY

Stephan, a guest on the Fathering Strong Podcast, shared a powerful story of how faith and action intertwined during his daughter's battle with addiction. "Every morning began with prayer – for strength, wisdom, and hope," he recalled. "Then I'd spend hours calling treatment centers, researching programs, and doing whatever I could to help her." Like the persistent widow Jesus spoke of in Luke 18, Stephan never gave up. His faith wasn't passive; it manifested in countless phone calls, sleepless nights researching options, and unwavering advocacy for his daughter. "I believed in miracles," he told me, his voice thick with emotion, "but I also believed God gave me the strength to be her warrior, her advocate, her father." His story beautifully illustrates how faith bridges the gap between prayer and persistent action, showing that true fortitude often means combining steadfast belief with determined effort.

The beauty of this faith-action dynamic lies in its ripple effects. When our children witness us actively living out our faith – especially during life's storms – we teach them that spirituality isn't just about Sunday services or bedtime prayers. It's about allowing our faith to fuel our actions, even when the path ahead seems impossible. As Paul writes in Philippians 4:13, "I can do all this through him who gives me strength." – not through passive waiting, but through active engagement with life's challenges.

BUILDING YOUR FORTITUDE

Looking back at that night in the ENT's office with my son, I now understand that it was more than just a medical consultation – it was my initiation into the deeper meaning of fatherhood. Each monthly visit, each sleepless night holding him while he cried in pain, each worried conversation with doctors had been building my fortitude without my realizing it. My wife and I asked many questions, and guided by our faith, we decided to wait a few more months before making a final decision about the ear tubes. Through God's grace, that was the last time he experienced ear infections, and the surgery was never needed.

Through this experience, I learned that fortitude isn't just about making tough decisions – it's about having the patience and wisdom to know when to wait, when to act, and when to trust in a higher power. Sometimes the strongest choice we can make as fathers is to step back, listen carefully, and let our faith guide us through uncertainty.

Like the fathers whose stories I've shared, I discovered that true strength often lies in knowing when to pause and reflect rather than rushing into action. Their examples, combined with my own journey, taught me an invaluable lesson: fortitude requires both the courage to act and the wisdom to wait.

That's the heart of fortitude – not the absence of fear or struggle, but the presence of something stronger: love. Every father's story I've shared points to this same truth. We persist not because we're strong enough on our own but because the love we have for our children makes us stronger than we ever thought possible.

In the end, fortitude isn't just about weathering life's storms – it's about the legacy we leave in their wake. Our children may not remember every sacrifice, every long night, every extra shift we worked, but they will remember how we faced life's challenges. They will carry with them the quiet strength they witnessed in our persistence, the steadfast love they saw in our presence, and the living faith they observed in our actions.

This is the gift of fortitude: not that we shield our children from life's difficulties, but that we show them how to face them with grace, grit, and unwavering hope. And perhaps, years from now, when they face their own storms, they'll remember watching their father stand tall against the wind, and they'll know they can do the same.

REFLECTIVE QUESTIONS ON BUILDING FORTITUDE

1. Think about a recent challenge you faced as a father. What inner resources did you draw upon to handle it? How might those same resources serve you in future difficulties?
2. When was the last time you felt like giving up? What or who helped you persevere? How can you build a stronger support system for the challenges ahead?
3. Consider a moment when your children witnessed you handling adversity. What message do you think your response sent them? How might you handle a similar situation differently next time?
4. In what areas of fatherhood do you feel most vulnerable? How might reframing these vulnerabilities as opportunities for growth change your perspective?
5. Write about a time when your faith or personal beliefs helped you overcome a parenting challenge. How can you actively strengthen this spiritual or emotional foundation?

6. Who are the father figures in your life who modeled fortitude? What specific lessons about resilience did they teach you, and how are you passing these lessons on to your children?
7. What daily habits or practices could you develop to build your emotional and mental stamina for fatherhood's challenges?
8. Think about a current struggle you're facing. What would handling this situation with fortitude look like? What's one step you could take today toward that goal?
9. How do you define success as a father? How might this definition be holding you back or pushing you forward?
10. What legacy of resilience do you want to leave for your children? What actions can you take this week to begin building that legacy?

Take time to journal your responses to these questions. Remember, building fortitude is like building muscle - it requires regular exercise, reflection, and rest. Consider discussing your answers with other fathers who can relate to your journey and offer their own insights and experiences.

CHAPTER 5

FAITH - THE ANCHORING STRENGTH OF A FATHERING STRONG LIFE

I'll never forget the morning I found my daughter's college application essay crumpled in the trash. She had been struggling with self-doubt about her future, questioning her worth and abilities. As I smoothed out those wrinkled pages and read her words, I felt my heart breaking. In that moment, like countless others in my fatherhood journey, faith became my anchor. It wasn't just about praying for her confidence – it was about finding strength in knowing that something greater than myself could guide us both through this valley of uncertainty.

In the journey of fatherhood, we all face moments that test our limits. Whether it's a health crisis, a rebellious teenager, or the daily grind of balancing work and family, it's easy to feel overwhelmed. That's where faith comes in. And I'm not just talking about following a specific religion or set of doctrines – though that may be part of your journey. I'm talking about cultivating a deep-rooted belief in something greater than ourselves, a source of strength that carries us through our toughest days.

WHY FAITH MATTERS IN FATHERHOOD

Faith isn't just a personal belief; it's a transformative force that shapes every aspect of fatherhood. I've witnessed this firsthand through countless stories in our Fathering Strong community. Take Tom, a single father of three, who shared how his faith helped him navigate a bitter divorce with grace. "When anger threatened to overwhelm me," he explained, "my faith reminded me to choose love instead. It became my moral compass when everything else felt chaotic."

The power of faith as a guide for ethical decision-making became clear when my daughter asked why we regularly help homeless men outside our grocery store. My faith provided the framework to explain human dignity and compassion in terms she could understand. Similarly, Tom's story demonstrates faith's role in fostering hope and resilience. When he lost his job during the pandemic, his unwavering faith not only sustained him but taught his children that setbacks are temporary. Today, he runs a successful small business, having transformed his challenge into a powerful lesson about perseverance.

During my own father's battle with cancer, faith became our family's anchor. It helped us find meaning in suffering and gave us strength to support each other through the darkest days. This experience showed my children how faith provides inner strength during life's toughest battles. In our daily lives, faith cultivates humility and gratitude through simple practices, like our evening dinner ritual of sharing three blessings from our day. This practice has profoundly impacted how my children view both their challenges and their blessings, helping them understand their connection to something greater than themselves.

FAITH IN ACTION: REAL STORIES FROM REAL FATHERS

Consider Jacob, a father of two teenagers. Every morning before school, he takes five minutes to pray with his kids. "It started when Sarah was struggling with bullying," he explains. "Those morning prayers became our way to face challenges together and remind ourselves that we're never alone."

Or take David, who lost his wife to cancer three years ago. His faith not only carried him through grief but helped him show his children how to find hope in life's darkest moments. Every Saturday, he and his kids volunteer at the same hospice center where their mother spent her final days, turning their pain into purpose.

Then there's Joshua, a firefighter and father of three, who relies on his faith during long, dangerous shifts. "Before each call, I say a quick prayer," he shares. "My kids know that faith gives me courage, and it teaches them that being brave doesn't mean not being scared – it means facing those fears with something stronger than fear." Joshua started a prayer circle at his station, which has since become a source of strength for many first-responder families in our community.

A young father, Alex, discovered the power of faith when his son was diagnosed with autism. "Faith gave me patience I didn't know I had," he admits. "It helped me see that every small victory – every word learned, every new skill mastered – was a blessing to be celebrated." Alex has now started to mentor other fathers of children with special needs, sharing how faith can transform challenges into opportunities for deeper connection and understanding.

ANCIENT WISDOM FOR MODERN FATHERS

These modern stories of fatherhood echo the timeless wisdom found in biblical narratives. Consider Abraham's unwavering faith through his trials, teaching us about trust in uncertain times. Or Joseph, who demonstrated unconditional love and forgiveness toward his brothers, modeling how modern fathers can navigate complex family dynamics. The prodigal son's father shows us the power of patience and unconditional love – qualities especially crucial in today's fast-paced, often-judgmental world.

The Bible's guidance on fatherhood remains remarkably relevant. Ephesians 6:4 advises fathers not to provoke their children to anger but to bring them up in discipline and instruction. This ancient wisdom perfectly aligns with modern parenting challenges, like Tom's conscious choice to respond with love during his divorce. Similarly, Psalm 103:13's description of a father's compassion provides a blueprint for fathers like Mike, who demonstrated resilience and faith during job loss.

These biblical principles don't just provide abstract guidance – they offer practical frameworks for modern fatherhood. They remind us that faith-based parenting isn't about perfection but about consistent love, guidance, and presence in our children's lives.

THE POWER OF FAITH IN OUR FATHERHOOD JOURNEY

As we've seen through these stories, faith isn't just a concept – it's a living, breathing force that transforms how we approach fatherhood. It's the quiet strength that steadies our hand when signing school forms and the mighty courage that helps us face life's biggest storms. Whether it manifests through prayer, meditation, service to others, or simply a deep-seated belief in something greater than ourselves, faith provides the foundation upon which we build our legacy as fathers.

Remember, faith doesn't make the path easier, but when combined with courage, fortitude, and love, it creates an unshakeable foundation for fatherhood. Faith gives us the wisdom to know when to stand firm, courage provides the strength to face our fears, fortitude helps us persevere through challenges, and love guides our every action. Together, these virtues remind us that we're not alone in this sacred task of raising our children. There's divine purpose in our struggles and eternal meaning in our sacrifices. As we continue our fatherhood journey, let these four pillars be our compass, guiding us toward the kind of fathers we aspire to be – men who lead with unwavering love, serve with steadfast courage, persevere with remarkable fortitude, and face each day with deep, abiding faith in the future we're building for our children.

REFLECTIVE QUESTIONS FOR YOUR FAITH JOURNEY

1. When was the last time you had to rely completely on faith to make a difficult parenting decision, and what did that experience teach you about trusting in something greater than yourself?

2. How has your understanding of faith evolved since becoming a father? What beliefs or practices have become more meaningful or changed entirely?

3. In what ways do you actively demonstrate your faith to your children beyond traditional religious practices? How do they respond to these demonstrations?

4. Think about a moment when your faith was severely tested as a father. How did you maintain your spiritual strength, and what did your children learn from watching you navigate that challenge?

5. What spiritual or faith-based traditions have you created specifically for your family? How have these traditions strengthened your bond with your children?

6. How do you reconcile moments when your faith seems to conflict with your children's developing beliefs or questions? What have these moments taught you about both faith and fatherhood?

7. In what ways has your faith helped you forgive yourself for your parenting mistakes? How has this self-forgiveness influenced your relationship with your children?

8. Think about the faith legacy you received from your own father. What aspects do you want to pass on to your children, and what aspects have you chosen to modify or leave behind?

9. How does your faith guide you in setting boundaries and making disciplinary decisions with your children? What principles from your faith inform these choices?

10. When you envision the spiritual or faith journey you hope your children will experience, what role do you see yourself playing in that journey? How are you preparing yourself for that role?

Take time to journal your responses to these questions. Your answers may reveal patterns, strengths, and areas where you can grow both as a father and in your faith journey.

CHAPTER 6

LOVE - THE HEART OF FATHERING STRONG

When my kids were growing up, I used to stay late at work once a week and wait for my son to finish his martial arts lessons. I was usually exhausted after a full day of work and tempted to head home, knowing my wife could pick him up instead. But then I remembered what my own father always said: "Love shows up." So many times, I would walk into the gym to let him know I was waiting, and the smile that lit up my son's face when he saw me reminded me why I was there. This moment captures the essence of what we've been exploring throughout this book – the core virtues of Fathering Strong. While courage, fortitude, and faith are crucial, there's one virtue that fuels them all: love. As 1 Corinthians 16:14 reminds us, "Do everything in love."

Think of Stan, a father who, after his divorce, moved across town but still drove 45 minutes each way, twice a week, to have breakfast with his daughters before school. "Some mornings, I'm running on empty," he told me, "but when I see their faces light up as I walk into that diner, I know this is what love looks like." Stan's story illustrates how love isn't just a feeling – it's action, commitment, and sometimes sacrifice.

LOVE: THE SOURCE OF ALL STRENGTH

One of my most vivid childhood memories is when my father spent a weekend building a treehouse for my sisters and me. While I mainly watched and fetched tools, Dad did most of the heavy lifting. That weekend taught me so much, and I spent countless hours playing in that treehouse throughout my youth. This memory perfectly captures what I've learned from my father and other father figures over the decades: love isn't just a warm, fuzzy feeling; it's a verb. It's action, commitment, and sometimes even a sore back.

As Pastor Eli Williams so powerfully writes in "Father Love - The Powerful Resource Every Child Needs," (Williams 2016) a father's love is as essential as the air our children breathe. I've seen this truth firsthand, both in my personal journey and through countless stories from other dads. When we love our children deeply, we give them an unshakeable foundation of security and self-worth that shapes their entire future.

Just yesterday, I watched a father in a local coffee shop sit patiently with his son working through math homework. No checking his phone, no multitasking – just fully present, offering encouraging words when frustration set in. This is exactly what Williams means when he emphasizes that love isn't just about words; it's about showing up, staying present, and walking alongside our children through both victories and struggles.

In my years of fathering, being associated with many men's groups and building the Fathering Strong communities, I've collected countless stories that showcase this love in action. Each one reminds me of how love transforms ordinary moments into lasting impacts:

> There's Steve, who rearranged his entire work schedule to coach his daughter's soccer team. "Some days I'm exhausted," he told me, "but watching her confidence grow with each practice makes it all worthwhile." This is love in action.
> I think of Carlos, who sits every evening with his teenage son, phones away, just listening. "Most nights he barely says a word," Carlos shared, "but when he needs to talk, he knows I'm there." This is love in action.

- Stan's story always moves me – working days at the office and nights driving Uber just so his kids can stay in their school after the divorce. "I'm tired," he admits, "but their stability comes first." This is love in action.
- I'll never forget Mark's courage in our father's group, sharing how he apologized to his daughter after losing his temper. "It was hard admitting I was wrong," he said, "but showing her that even fathers make mistakes – that felt like real strength." This is love in action.
- And there's David, whose fierce advocacy for his son with autism inspires us all. Meeting after meeting, expert after expert, never giving up until his boy got the support he needed. This is love in action.

These stories, each unique yet connected by the thread of father-love, lead us to understand an even deeper truth about fatherhood – love isn't just the foundation of our actions, it's the driving force behind everything we do as fathers.

LOVE: THE DRIVING FORCE BEHIND FATHERING STRONG

Love isn't just one of the virtues of Fathering Strong - it's the driving force behind them all. When we talk about being better fathers, showing up for our children, creating lasting bonds, and building meaningful memories, everything circles back to love. This fundamental force motivates us to wake up early for soccer practice, sit patiently through homework struggles, celebrate small victories, and provide comfort during tough times.

Love gives us the courage to face our fears and stand up for what's right. It powers us through challenges and keeps us going when we feel overwhelmed. It strengthens our faith, deepening our trust in God's guidance during uncertain times. Without love, these virtues become empty obligations, missing the warmth and genuine connection that make parenting truly meaningful.

A father can provide material comforts and set boundaries, but these actions feel mechanical without love as their foundation. Love transforms routine parental duties into precious moments of connection. It turns discipline into gentle guidance and everyday conversations into treasured memories. When children feel deeply loved, they develop the emotional security and confidence to thrive, and someday, they'll carry this gift of love forward to their own children.

Pastor Bob, who leads a local congregation, often shares about his journey raising his son with autism. "There were days," he says, "when I felt completely inadequate, but love gave me the strength to learn, to adapt, and to be the father my son needed." His experience echoes what Pastor Eli Williams articulates in "Father Love - The Powerful Resource Every Child Needs." "A father's love isn't just desirable – it's as essential as food and shelter."

I witnessed this truth firsthand when coaching my daughter's soccer team. One rainy Saturday, Sarah, one of our players, took a hard fall. Her father, Jacob, who rarely missed a game despite working night shifts, immediately rushed to her side. He didn't just help her up; he spent the next ten minutes walking the sideline with her, encouraging her until she felt ready to play again. That's love in action – present, patient, and persistent.

The Bible reminds us of this transformative power in 1 John 4:18: "Perfect love drives out fear." I've seen this verse come alive through fathers like Andy, who adopted three siblings from foster care. Despite the challenges of helping these children heal from past trauma, Andy's persistent love gradually broke through their walls of fear and distrust. "Every time they tested my love," he tells other fathers, "I just loved them more firmly, more intentionally." Today, those children are thriving – a testament to love's power to strengthen not just the giver, but the receiver as well.

In one of the Fathering Strong polls, we asked fathers to identify their greatest source of strength in parenting. While answers vary from faith to community support, they all circle back to one truth: **love empowers us to push beyond our perceived limitations.** As the apostle Paul writes in Ephesians 3:17-19, we are "rooted and established in love" – a foundation that enables us to accomplish more than we ever thought possible in our role as fathers.

LOVE: THE LEGACY WE LEAVE

Many years ago, at my grandfather's funeral, person after person stood up to share stories about how his consistent love had touched their lives. One young man, now a father himself, spoke through tears about how my granddad had stepped in to mentor him through high school after losing his own father. Years later when our paths crossed again, his eyes welled up as he told me, "Your grandfather showed me what it means to love like a dad. Now I'm passing those same lessons on to my own kids."

During the reception at my dad's funeral a few years ago, my sister shared a story that touched my heart. While battling postpartum depression, she revealed how Dad had silently rearranged his schedule to bring her lunch every Wednesday. He never drew attention to these visits or made them feel like a burden – he simply appeared at her door, week after week, ensuring she had both food and companionship. Now, years later, she carries on his legacy by doing the same for new mothers in her community, quietly extending that circle of care and understanding. Even after his passing, Dad's simple act of love continues to ripple outward, touching lives he never knew he'd reach.

This is the ripple effect that Pastor Eli Williams describes in his work – how a father's love extends far beyond his immediate family, touching future generations. When we demonstrate love daily through our actions, whether in our marriages, our relationships with our children, or our service to others, we create a legacy that truly matters.

Remember, love isn't just the heart of Fathering Strong – it's the heartbeat of every strong father. It's what gets us up early for those soccer games, keeps us patient during homework struggles, and helps us persist through our children's challenging seasons. As you continue your fatherhood journey, **let love be your guide, your strength, and your motivation.**

A FATHER'S PRAYER OF LOVE

Heavenly Father,

Grant us the strength to love like You love – consistently, unconditionally, and without reservation. Help us remember that in our weakest moments, when patience runs thin and energy fades, Your perfect love can flow through our imperfect efforts.

Give us the wisdom to show up when it matters most, the courage to love even when it's difficult, and the perseverance to keep loving through every season of our children's lives. Let our love be more than words – make it visible in our actions, evident in our choices, and felt in our presence.

May our children look back one day and say, "My father's love made me stronger." And may that love ripple outward, touching not just our own families but future generations we may never meet.

Guide us in leaving a legacy of love that honors You and shapes the future of fatherhood. In Your strong and loving name we pray,

Amen.

QUESTIONS FOR REFLECTION: LOVE IN YOUR FATHERHOOD JOURNEY

1. When was the last time you let your daily responsibilities slide to be fully present with your child? What did that moment teach you about love's priorities?

2. Think of a time when loving your child felt difficult or challenging. How did you push through, and what did that experience reveal about your capacity to love?

3. In what ways does your expression of love differ from how your father showed love to you? How has this shaped your approach to fathering?

4. Consider your child's love language. Are you showing love in ways that speak to their heart, or are you defaulting to what feels natural to you?

5. When have you chosen love over pride in your parenting? What did that decision cost you, and what did it gain?

6. How do you demonstrate love during moments of discipline? What messages do your actions send about the relationship between love and boundaries?

7. Think about your daily routine. Where could you create more intentional moments of connection and love with your children?

8. In what ways has your understanding of love evolved since becoming a father? How has this growth changed your parenting approach?

9. When your child is struggling, how do you balance protecting them with letting them learn through difficulty? How does love guide this decision?

10. Looking ahead, what legacy of love do you want to leave for your children? What specific actions can you take today to build that legacy?

Take time to journal your responses to these questions. Your answers may reveal patterns, opportunities for growth, and beautiful truths about your journey in father-love that you hadn't noticed before.

PART 2

FROM FOUNDATION TO ACTION: BUILDING YOUR FATHERING STRONG BLUEPRINT

In Part 1, we explored the four core virtues of Fathering Strong: courage, fortitude, faith, and love. Now, Part 2 shows you how to transform these core virtues into practical action across six foundational strengths of fatherhood:

- **Personal Health:** Build physical strength and vitality through courage and fortitude
- **Spiritual Health:** Deepen your spiritual foundation through active faith
- **Emotional Wealth:** Develop emotional intelligence by combining love and courage
- **Financial Wealth:** Practice sound financial stewardship through fortitude and faith
- **Marriage:** Create an unshakeable partnership by blending love with courage
- **Connection with Children:** Foster lasting family bonds through faith and love

In each chapter, you'll receive three powerful tools:

1. **Goal-Setting Strategies:** Practical frameworks for creating meaningful change
2. **Tangible Examples:** Real stories from fathers who've successfully applied these principles
3. **SMART Goals:** Clear examples of specific, measurable objectives for each area

We'll begin with a crucial chapter on goal-setting—the bridge that turns noble intentions into real results. As Proverbs 16:3 teaches us, "Commit to the Lord whatever you do, and he will establish your plans." You'll learn to transform broad aspirations like "being more present" into specific, actionable steps using the SMART framework (Specific, Measurable, Achievable, Relevant, and Time-bound).

By the end of Part 2, you'll have more than just inspiration—you'll have a detailed roadmap for becoming the father you want to be. Each virtue from Part 1 will come alive through practical, everyday actions that strengthen your family bonds.

Let's turn those core virtues into life-changing habits that will shape your family's future.

CHAPTER 7

SETTING YOUR COURSE -
HOW GOALS MAKE YOU STRONGER

I'll never forget the day my son asked me, "Dad, where are we going?" We were hiking at one of our local nature reserves, and I had confidently led us off the main trail, insisting I knew a shortcut. A half-hour later, we were completely lost. That moment taught me more than just the importance of bringing a map—it showed me how much our children depend on us to have direction and purpose.

Many of us fathers feel like I did that day: convinced we're heading somewhere good but really just wandering without clear direction. We wake up, go to work, come home, and repeat—hoping we're doing enough for our families but never quite sure.

This section of the book is about finding your path and setting goals that will help you become the father God created you to be. When I started my fatherhood journey, I thought love and good intentions were enough. But as a pastor once told me, "A ship without a destination will never reach port." Through incorporating the virtues of courage, fortitude, faith, and love into specific goals, I discovered a way to transform good intentions into real growth and lasting impact.

Our earliest experiences shape our understanding of fatherhood, whether through positive role models or their absence. My own father, despite his imperfections, showed his love through consistent presence— attending my sports games, teaching practical skills, and offering spiritual guidance. Research confirms that this kind of intentional parenting pays dividends: studies show that individuals who pursue clear personal goals not only experience greater happiness and well-being but also enjoy better physical health (Emmons 105-128). Whether you had a strong father figure or not, setting deliberate goals today can help you become the parent your children need—and perhaps the father you always wished you'd had.

WHY GOALS MATTER

I've learned that while most of us understand the value of setting goals, very few actually put this knowledge into practice. It's like knowing the trail map exists but never taking it out of your pocket. When I finally started writing down my goals and sharing them with a trusted friend, everything changed. Studies back this up—research from Michigan State (Traugott 2014) shows that people who write down their goals and share their progress are nearly twice as likely to achieve them than those who keep their aims to themselves.

I wish I'd known this earlier in my fatherhood journey. Like many dads, I spent years operating on autopilot, assuming my good intentions would somehow translate into being the father I wanted to be. But just as I learned on that nature trail with my son, good intentions without clear direction often leave us lost.

When I finally started setting specific fatherhood goals, they became my compass. Each morning, I woke up with purpose, knowing exactly what steps I needed to take to become a better dad. These goals weren't just items on a to-do list—they were promises to my children, commitments to the kind of father I wanted to be. And, they are the reason this book actually made it to print!

Think of goals as your map and compass on this journey of fatherhood. They help you navigate the challenging waters ahead, keeping you focused on what truly matters instead of drifting with the current of daily distractions. And just like any meaningful journey, becoming the father God created you to be happens one step at a time, one goal at a time.

THE SMART APPROACH TO GOAL SETTING

I first encountered SMART goals in my corporate job, which we used for everything from quarterly sales targets to project deadlines. It didn't take long for me to realize these same principles could transform my approach to fatherhood. This isn't just another acronym—it's a proven path that helped me turn my good intentions into real action. Let me share what I've learned about making goals that stick.

First, make your goals **Specific**. I used to say things like "I want to be more present for my kids." But that was too vague. When I changed it to "I will put my phone away and spend 30 minutes playing with my children after dinner," everything shifted. I knew exactly what I needed to do.

Your goals need to be **Measurable**—you need clear metrics to track your progress. Instead of saying "I want to be more involved in my kids' lives," I started counting the number of one-on-one conversations I had with each child per week. I tracked how many family dinners we shared together each month. I even kept a log of the activities we did together on weekends. When my daughter wanted to learn piano, I set a goal to practice with her three times per week and tracked our sessions in a simple chart on the fridge. These concrete numbers showed me exactly where I stood and motivated me to keep improving.

The A stands for **Achievable**. I learned this the hard way when I promised to coach three different sports teams in one season. It wasn't realistic with my work schedule, and I ended up disappointing everyone. Now I set goals I can actually reach, even if they stretch me a bit.

Relevant goals align with your values as a father. Each goal should reflect what matters most to you and your family. When I set goals that connected with my deeper purpose—like teaching my son to pray or helping my daughter build confidence—I found myself more motivated to follow through.

Finally, **Time-bound** goals give your aspirations a deadline and create momentum. When my daughter expressed interest in swimming, saying "I'll teach her someday" wasn't enough. Instead, I committed: "By the end of summer, she will be able to swim one lap independently." Having that deadline pushed me to schedule weekly pool visits and track her progress. Without a timeframe, even our best intentions can drift endlessly. Whether it's teaching your son to tie his shoes by his first day of kindergarten or establishing a weekly family game night by next month, setting clear deadlines turns dreams into action.

PUTTING SMART GOALS INTO PRACTICE

In the next six chapters, we'll explore how SMART goals can transform different areas of your life as a father. Just like that day hiking and getting lost taught me the importance of having clear direction (and paying attention to the trail markers), I've learned that setting proper goals is about more than just having good intentions—it's about creating a map for the journey ahead.

Let me give you a simple example. When my son was struggling with reading, saying, "I need to help him read better," wasn't enough. Instead, I set a SMART goal: "I will read with my son for 15 minutes every night before bedtime for the next month." This goal gave me a clear path forward, and within weeks, I could see his confidence growing.

In the coming chapters, we'll dive deep into six crucial areas where SMART goals can strengthen your fatherhood journey:

- ‣ Physical Strength
- ‣ Spiritual Strength
- ‣ Emotional Wealth
- ‣ Financial Wealth

- ▸ Spouse Relationship
- ▸ Children Bonding

For each area, I'll share specific examples of SMART goals that have worked for me and other fathers that have shared their stories. You'll learn how to transform vague intentions like "be a better dad" or "get in shape" into concrete, achievable goals that will help you become the father God created you to be.

In Part 3 of the book is where we will take these SMART goals and develop an actionable, meaningful plan equipped with all the tools you need for success. You'll receive practical worksheets, tracking templates, and accountability strategies that have helped countless fathers turn their goals into lasting change. This isn't just about setting goals—it's about creating a sustainable path to becoming the father your family deserves.

Remember, just as I needed that map on hiking adventure, you need clear direction to reach your destination. SMART goals provide that direction, turning your fatherhood aspirations into reality. As we explore each area in the upcoming chapters, you'll discover how to create goals that will guide you toward becoming the father your children need.

REFLECTION QUESTIONS FOR BUILDING YOUR BLUEPRINT

1. What legacy do you want to leave for your children, and how can setting specific goals help shape that legacy?
2. Think of a time when you felt most fulfilled as a father. What specific actions or behaviors led to that moment, and how could you turn those into regular goals?
3. If your children were to describe you to their own kids someday, what would you want them to say? What goals would help make that vision a reality?

4. What's one area of fatherhood where you feel you're currently "wandering without a map"? How might setting clear goals in this area change your family's trajectory?
5. Consider your own father (or father figure). What positive traits would you like to emulate, and what aspects would you like to do differently? How can you translate these reflections into concrete goals?
6. What obstacles or fears have prevented you from setting clear fatherhood goals in the past? How might naming these barriers help you overcome them?
7. If you could guarantee success in just one area of fatherhood this year, what would it be? Why does this particular area matter so much to you?
8. How might your relationship with your children change if you approached fatherhood with the same intentionality you bring to your career or other important life goals?
9. What daily habits or patterns currently pull you away from being the father you want to be? What specific goals could help redirect your time and energy?
10. When you imagine yourself five years from now, what kind of relationship do you want to have with your children? What steps can you start taking today to build that future?

Take time to journal your answers to these questions. Your responses will serve as foundational material as we begin crafting your personal fatherhood goals in the coming chapters.

CHAPTER 8

PHYSICAL HEALTH - FUELING YOUR BODY AND MIND

When my kids were young, I learned a hard lesson about physical health. After another exhausting day of trying to keep up with their endless energy, I found myself collapsing on the couch instead of joining their playground adventures. That's when it hit me: being a strong father isn't just about showing up – it's about having the physical energy to be fully present for your family.

In Fathering Strong, we view physical health as more than just exercise routines or diet plans. It's about building the strength and vitality you need to be the dad your family deserves. Think about your typical day: from morning roughhousing with your toddler to coaching evening soccer practice, your body needs to keep up with the demands of active fatherhood. When you're constantly battling fatigue or health issues, it affects everything – your patience, your presence, and even your ability to engage meaningfully with your spouse and children.

THE ESSENTIAL COMPONENTS OF PHYSICAL STRENGTH AND TOTAL WELLNESS

Twenty-five years ago, I struggled just like many other dads - overwhelmed, trying to balance family life while staying healthy. That personal challenge, combined with my belief that there had to be a better way to maintain health as we age, inspired me to create the Lifegevity program (Stapleton, Lifegevity Wellness Program 2011). What started as my own journey to better health evolved into a proven system that's now helped countless others live longer, more vibrant lives.

Here's what shocked me most during my research: While everyone obsesses over diet and exercise, they aren't actually the most important factors for lasting health. Through my work with hundreds of participants and The Canadian Institute of Stress, I discovered something unexpected - learning to relax, setting clear goals, and managing stress have an even greater impact. In this chapter, we'll explore what I call the Lifegevity Blueprint- the powerful interplay between exercise, nutrition, and relaxation that creates optimal health when working in harmony. We'll tackle goal-setting and stress management in later chapters, where we can give these crucial topics the attention they deserve.

PHYSICAL FITNESS: FINDING YOUR PATH TO STRENGTH

I remember the day I realized I needed to change my approach to exercise. My youngest son had asked me to play soccer in the backyard, and after just fifteen minutes, I was gasping for air and ready to quit. The look of disappointment on his face hit me like a gut punch. That moment taught me something crucial: as fathers, exercise isn't about getting six-pack abs or bench-pressing 250 pounds - it's about being able to say "yes" when our kids want to play.

Through developing the Lifegevity program, I've worked with hundreds of dads who've shared similar wake-up calls. What I discovered was that the best exercise program is one that prepares you for the everyday physical demands of fatherhood. Sometimes, that means having the stamina to chase a toddler around the house for hours; other times, it's having the energy to teach your teenager how to shoot hoops on a hot afternoon. The goal isn't perfection - it's being ready for these precious moments with your family.

When I first started helping others improve their overall wellness, I noticed a consistent pattern: they'd either focus entirely on one type of exercise (usually whatever they enjoyed in high school) or try to do everything at once and quickly burn out. Through research conducted by the Canadian Institute of Stress (Earle 1989) and my own studies with program participants, I've found that the sweet spot lies in a balanced approach.

I had a client, Jim, who was obsessed with improving his treadmill time during every session. His focus was purely on performance metrics rather than health benefits. He'd get so caught up in adjusting his headphones and finding the perfect workout music that he nearly tumbled off the treadmill multiple times.

When I showed him that his heart rate was consistently exceeding his recommended training zone, I explained that this time should be used for building cardiovascular health, preferably without headphones. Jim looked at me in disbelief and replied, "I was a marine and was taught no pain, no gain!"

Initially, he was resistant to the idea of exercising without his music. However, after some convincing, he agreed to try it for a few days. About a week later, while he was on the treadmill, he shared something interesting: "I just came up with a great new program for my business while I was on the treadmill."

"Great." I responded, "It sounds like you finally got the hang of what you need to do and are seeing the benefits." After that, Jim never mentioned missing his music again.

FATHER FITNESS: BUILDING COMPLETE STRENGTH

Think of your body like a car that needs to run reliably for your family every single day. You need:

> - A well-tuned engine (cardiovascular fitness)
> - Strong horsepower (strength training)
> - Smooth handling (flexibility training)

Skip any one of these, and like a car with poor maintenance, your body will start breaking down. I learned this lesson the hard way when my daughter challenged me to a race in the backyard. She had just started track and was feeling confident. "Dad, I bet I can beat you to the fence!" she said, her eyes sparkling with competitive spirit. Having been a college athlete, and seeing that the fence was only about 30 yards away, I thought this would be easy.

"Go!" she shouted, and we both took off. After about five steps, I felt a sharp pain in my groin - I had pulled a muscle, and it hurt badly. Needless to say, my daughter won the race. While I had been exercising regularly, I was only focusing on strength training and had completely neglected flexibility. Now I was paying the price.

That humbling experience taught me an important lesson: true fitness isn't about excelling in just one area - it's about building a foundation that supports all aspects of dad life. My pulled muscle wasn't just about missing flexibility work; it was a wake-up call to approach fitness more holistically.

Let's look at each part of the three key components of staying fit through the lens of real dad life.

CARDIOVASCULAR FITNESS: YOUR DAILY ENERGY ENGINE

Remember that feeling of being out of breath after chasing your toddler for just a few minutes? That's your cardiovascular system asking for attention. I used to think I was too busy for cardio until I started turning everyday dad moments into heart-healthy opportunities. Walking to school with my kids instead of driving, dancing in the living room during commercial breaks, or playing tag in the backyard - these all count. The key isn't running marathons (unless that's your thing); it's about building enough endurance to keep up with your kids' energy levels.

STRENGTH TRAINING: POWER FOR DAILY DAD DUTIES

One of my clients once told me, "I didn't think I needed strength training until I couldn't lift my sleeping six-year-old from the car to bed." Being strong isn't about bulging biceps - it's about handling the physical demands of fatherhood with confidence. Whether you're lifting car seats, carrying groceries while holding a baby, or becoming your kids' favorite jungle gym, strength matters. You don't need a fancy gym membership; your body weight, resistance bands, or even filled water bottles can work as weights when you're starting out.

During a fitness talk I was giving, someone asked me, "What's the best piece of exercise equipment you can use?" I replied with a smile, "The one that you actually use!" After all, even the most expensive equipment is worthless if it just becomes an expensive clothes hanger.

FLEXIBILITY: THE OFTEN FORGOTTEN FOUNDATION

Here's a truth I learned too late: flexibility isn't just for yoga enthusiasts - it's a crucial dad skill. It's what lets you drop to the floor for an impromptu tea party with your toddler and pop back up without sounding like a rusty hinge. It's about twisting yourself into a pretzel to wrestle with those stubborn car seat buckles or crouching down to tie tiny shoes without your spine filing a formal complaint. And trust me, you'll want that flexibility when your daughter challenges you to a spontaneous race across the playground - because nothing ruins your "World's Most Fun Dad" reputation quite like having to decline due to a pulled groin muscle!

Simple stretching before bed, basic yoga poses, or even playing "follow the leader" with your kids (bonus: they'll think you're just having fun) can keep you limber and ready for whatever fatherhood throws your way. And trust me, as you get older, this becomes even more important - especially when you're trying to keep up with energetic grandkids during floor time. Your future self will thank you for staying flexible now.

MAKING IT ALL WORK TOGETHER: A DAD'S GUIDE TO SUSTAINABLE FITNESS

Let me share a story that transformed how I teach fitness to fathers. Early in my career, I worked with a dad named Tom who repeatedly struggled with every workout program he attempted. His motivation wasn't the issue - the problem was that he viewed exercise as just another task on his to-do list, completely disconnected from his family time. Together, we uncovered something powerful: the most effective fitness routine for a dad is one that naturally blends into family life.

Here's what I've learned from working with hundreds of dads: forget about those intense 90-minute gym sessions if they don't fit your life. Instead, think smaller but smarter. I call it the "Father's Fitness Formula":

> **Look at what you're already doing** - it's a goldmine of fitness opportunities. Those weekly trips chasing your kids around the park? That's perfect cardio. Carrying your sleepy kids to bed? You've got built-in strength training right there.

> **Layer fitness into your daily routines.** I knock out pushups while my kids brush their teeth. Another dad I know cranks out squats during those 3 minutes waiting for baby bottles to warm. These small moments might seem trivial, but they stack up to make a real difference. After dinner walks or bike rides were always fun and a way to burn off the kids extra energy before bed.

> **Get the kids involved.** My biggest breakthrough came when I stopped treating exercise as solo "me time" and transformed it into family "we time. When my kids were little, I would lie on my back during their playtime. They'd climb on top of me, and I'd grab their hands and lift them up with my legs, flipping them over in a controlled somersault motion. They would squeal with delight and immediately want to do it again. Not only was I getting an incredible leg workout, but we were creating precious memories together.

THE REAL SECRET TO STICKING WITH IT

Here's what no fitness magazine will tell you: as a dad, your exercise routine will get interrupted. Kids get sick, work runs late, sleep becomes precious, and those perfectly planned workout schedules? They'll get shredded faster than your abs. **The key isn't perfection - it's persistence.**

I keep a "minimum viable workout" list on my phone: five minutes of basic exercises I can do anywhere, anytime. We're talking push-ups, squats, planks - nothing fancy, just the fundamentals. On good days, I do more. On tough days, I at least hit that minimum. And you know what? That's okay.

The reality of parenting is that some weeks you'll crush your fitness goals, and others you'll barely squeeze in those five minutes between diaper changes and deadline meetings. But those five minutes matter. They keep the habit alive. They remind your body and mind that fitness is still a priority, even if it's not always the top priority.

I've learned that consistency beats intensity every time. Those Instagram fitness influencers showing their two-hour gym sessions? That's great for them, but in dad-life, we need practical solutions. Sometimes your "gym" is your living room floor at 5:30 AM, and your "workout buddy" is a toddler using you as a jungle gym. Roll with it.

FUELING YOUR BODY: THE POWER OF NUTRITION

The food you eat directly impacts your strength and health. Your food choices affect your energy levels, mood, sleep quality, and overall well-being. As a father, healthy eating goes beyond taking care of yourself - it's about modeling good nutrition habits that your children will carry with them throughout their lives.

Let's talk about real-world energy foods that work for busy dads. These aren't fancy superfoods you need to hunt down at specialty stores - they're practical options you can grab at any grocery store:

- Oatmeal with berries: A bowl in the morning gives you steady energy for hours, plus it's something the kids will eat too
- Bananas: Nature's perfect snack - throw one in your work bag for a quick energy boost
- Greek yogurt with honey: Great protein hit, and the natural sugars help fuel your afternoon
- Trail mix: Keep some in your car or desk drawer - the nuts provide protein and healthy fats, while dried fruit gives you quick energy
- Hard-boiled eggs: Prep a batch on Sunday, and you've got protein-packed snacks ready all week

The key is having these foods readily available. When you're running on empty between meetings or chasing toddlers, you need fuel that's easy to grab and won't lead to a crash an hour later.

THE MACRONUTRIENT BALANCE: PROTEIN, CARBOHYDRATES, AND FATS

Your body needs three main types of nutrients to stay healthy: protein, carbohydrates, and fats. Here's what makes each one essential:

- **Protein:** This vital nutrient builds and repairs muscles, supports your immune system, and helps maintain strong bones. Find it in lean meats like chicken and fish, as well as eggs, dairy, beans, and nuts. Including protein in every meal helps your body stay strong and healthy.
- **Carbohydrates:** Your body's primary energy source. Choose nutrient-rich options like fresh fruits, colorful vegetables, and whole grains. These provide steady energy throughout the day, unlike sugary snacks and drinks that lead to energy crashes and unwanted weight gain.
- **Fats:** Essential for brain function, vitamin absorption, and overall health. Focus on heart-healthy sources like avocados, nuts, olive oil, and fatty fish such as salmon. Limit saturated fats from fatty meats and fried foods to protect your heart.

BALANCE AND MODERATION: THE KEYS
TO SUSTAINABLE NUTRITION

Healthy eating doesn't require strict diets or eliminating entire food groups. The key is finding an approach that works for your lifestyle and that you can maintain over time. Focus on enjoying a balanced mix of nutritious foods in moderate portions. This means incorporating plenty of vegetables, fruits, whole grains, lean proteins, and healthy fats into your daily meals.

While it's fine to treat yourself occasionally, make nutritious choices the foundation of your meals. There's no need to feel guilty about enjoying a slice of cake at a birthday party or having pizza with friends. The goal is progress, not perfection. What matters most is your overall eating pattern, not any single meal or day.

This sustainable approach makes healthy eating easier to maintain long-term and sets a positive example for your children. When kids see their parents making balanced food choices and having a healthy relationship with food, they're more likely to develop good eating habits themselves. Remember that small, consistent changes add up to significant improvements in your health over time.

LEADING YOUR FAMILY TO HEALTHY HABITS

Your children observe and mirror your behaviors, especially when it comes to food. The way you eat and think about nutrition will deeply influence their lifelong attitudes and habits. Consider these proven strategies to build healthy eating habits in your family:

- ▸ **Make family meals a priority**: Share regular meals together without phones, tablets, or TV to foster meaningful connections
- ▸ **Involve children in meal preparation**: Let them help with age-appropriate tasks like washing vegetables or measuring ingredients to build their interest in nutrition

- ▸ **Create a healthy food environment:** Stock nutritious snacks and minimize processed foods so better choices are always within reach
- ▸ **Model mindful eating:** Show your children how to enjoy food in moderation by eating slowly and paying attention to hunger cues
- ▸ **Teach nutrition fundamentals:** Help children understand how different foods fuel their bodies, giving them the energy to learn and play
- ▸ **Maintain neutral food relationships:** Avoid using food as rewards or punishments to prevent emotional eating habits

TOOLS FOR SUCCESS

Tracking your nutrition journey has never been easier, thanks to the wide variety of smartphone apps available today. These powerful tools can help you monitor your food intake, understand portion sizes, and make informed choices about your diet. Here are some of the most useful nutrition tracking apps:

- ▸ MyFitnessPal (myfitnesspal n.d.): Comprehensive food database with easy meal logging
- ▸ Lose It! (LoseIt! n.d.): Goal-focused tracking with personalized planning
- ▸ Cronometer (Cronometer n.d.): Detailed nutritional analysis including micronutrients
- ▸ Fooducate (Fooducate n.d.): Educational tool for understanding food quality and ingredients

While these tools can guide better choices, remember that perfect tracking isn't the goal. Focus instead on building sustainable, healthy habits that will inspire your children to do the same.

Strong fathers understand that nutrition isn't just about personal health - it's about leading by example and building a foundation of wellness for the entire family. Your food choices today shape your children's relationship with nutrition for years to come. When kids see

Dad making mindful decisions about meals, choosing fresh vegetables over processed snacks, and taking time to prepare wholesome food, they internalize these habits.

It's more than just what's on the dinner plate - it's about creating a positive food culture at home. By involving your children in meal planning, grocery shopping, and cooking, you're teaching them essential life skills while strengthening your bond. These moments in the kitchen become opportunities for connection and learning, where stories are shared and traditions are born.

Remember, your children are watching and learning from every choice you make. When they see you prioritizing nutritious meals and treating your body with respect, they're more likely to develop healthy eating habits that will serve them well throughout their lives. This is one of the most powerful gifts a father can give - the foundation for a lifetime of good health.

A FATHER'S GUIDE TO RELAXATION

"I'll rest when the kids are grown."

That was my motto for years, and I hear it from almost every dad I talk to. We wear our exhaustion like a badge of honor, convinced that constant motion equals good parenting. Then came my wake-up call - literally. At just 36 years old, I found myself driving to the ER, gripping the steering wheel, convinced I was having a heart attack. It turned out to be "just" a stress attack, but the message was clear. I had been burning the candle at both ends: working late, going in early, and desperately trying to be there for my kids all while running myself into the ground in the name of being a "good dad."

REDEFINING REST FOR REAL DADS

When most parenting books talk about relaxation, they suggest things like "take a peaceful bath" or "meditate for an hour." I can hear you laughing. With a toddler banging on the bathroom door or a teenager needing a ride to practice, traditional relaxation advice often feels like it was written for someone else's life.

But here's what I've learned: relaxation for fathers isn't about escaping our family life - it's about finding moments of peace within it. It's about learning to ease off the accelerator before you burn out the engine.

Think about bodybuilders - they see their biggest gains not during workouts but during rest periods. The same principle applies to stress. While some stress can be beneficial like during exercise, continuous stress without recovery turns those benefits into health risks.

One dad in the Lifegevity program captured it perfectly: "I used to think relaxation meant checking out and wasting time. Now I realize it means checking in with myself - which helps me stay present for my family and build the stamina I need."

You know, even God rested on the seventh day. It wasn't because He was tired - He was setting an example for us. Throughout the Bible, we see this pattern of work and rest. Jesus himself would often withdraw to quiet places to recharge, even in the midst of his busy ministry. When I first read Matthew 11:28- "Come to me, all you who are weary and burdened, and I will give you rest" - it hit me differently as a dad. It wasn't just spiritual advice; it was a practical reminder that rest isn't lazy - it's essential. If the Creator of the universe took time to rest, maybe we dads need to stop feeling guilty about taking a breather too.

Going back to the foot on the accelerator analogy: if you never take your foot off the accelerator while keeping your other foot on the brake, what happens? You burn out the engine. When we never take breaks:

> Our patience shortens (hello, dad-rage over small problems)
> Our energy tanks (goodbye, evening playtime)
> Our health suffers (welcome, stress-related issues and illnesses)

FINDING PEACE IN THE CHAOS: A DAD'S GUIDE TO REAL RELAXATION

Finding time to relax as a dad feels about as realistic as finding a quiet moment in Chuck E. Cheese. But here's the thing: relaxation doesn't have to mean hour-long meditation sessions or fancy spa retreats. It's about finding those small pockets of peace in your day-to-day life.

Technology can actually help here. I was skeptical at first, but apps like Calm (Calm n.d.) and Headspace (Headspace n.d.) have been game-changers for a lot of dads I know. They've got these quick guided sessions - some just 3-5 minutes long - that you can squeeze in anywhere. Think waiting in the school pickup line or those few minutes before a stressful meeting. These apps are like having a pocket-sized relaxation coach, keeping you accountable and helping you build that mental muscle of staying calm under pressure. I started using Calm a number of years ago. My wife also took up using the app and she continues to listen to it every morning. It is so important to her that she got upset one time when she realized she was not logged in for a number of sessions and they didn't count towards her daily totals. I had to remind her that the objective was to reduce stress not create more stress!

Let me share some real-world strategies that have worked for me and other dads. These aren't your typical "just meditate for an hour" suggestions - these are battle-tested techniques that fit into the chaos of dad life.

The Two-Minute Reset

Let me share my go-to strategy when I'm about to lose it. I call it the ***"Dad's Two-Minute Reset,"*** and I discovered it one day in my car after a challenging parent-teacher conference:

> ➤ One minute: Just sit and breathe (even if you're in the school parking lot)
> ➤ One minute: Name three things you're grateful for about your kids

Sounds simple, right? But this tiny practice has saved countless dad moments from turning into dad meltdowns.

The Commute Conversion

Turn your daily drive to and from work into peaceful relaxation time (how well this works may depend on your location and traffic conditions).

- No phone calls - keep it quiet
- Play your favorite music or podcast
- Use each red light as a reminder to take one deep breath

When You Really Need to Recharge

Sometimes you need more than quick fixes. Here's how to make it happen without the guilt:

- **Trade time with your spouse:** "I'll take the kids Saturday morning if I can have Sunday afternoon"
- **Create a relaxing environment wherever you are:** I keep a favorite playlist ready on my phone and a stress ball in my desk drawer

THE RIPPLE EFFECT: HOW YOUR CALM CHANGES YOUR FAMILY

Let me share a moment that changed everything for me. My daughter had drawn all over our newly painted walls. Pre-relaxation practice me would have exploded. But because I'd just taken ten minutes to decompress after work, I handled it differently. Instead of yelling, I took a breath and turned it into a teaching moment about where we do and don't create art. My daughter still remembers this as the day we started her "art gallery" (aka the fridge).

What changes when dads learn to relax? I've witnessed the profound impact a father's state of mind has on the entire family. Children are incredibly perceptive emotional sponges, and when you're stressed, they absorb your tension, learn that stress is the normal state of being, and often blame themselves for your mood. However, when you're relaxed, the dynamic shifts dramatically. Your children feel secure enough to be themselves, learn healthy ways to handle pressure and develop emotional intelligence by watching your example. This transformation in your emotional state creates a foundation for healthier family relationships and better emotional development in your children.

THE LEGACY OF A HEALTHY FATHER

Consider the stark contrast between our two potential selves as fathers. When we're stressed and depleted, we tend to be reactive and short-tempered, missing precious moments with our children. But when we're properly rested, we transform into patient, present parents who create lasting memories. This isn't about achieving perfect zen-like calm at all times – we're still human, after all. But even brief moments of intentional rest can turn bedtime battles into storytelling adventures, homework struggles into valuable teaching opportunities, and hectic morning rushes into meaningful bonding time.

HANDLING THE GUILT

One of the biggest obstacles fathers face when prioritizing relaxation is guilt - that nagging voice suggesting any moment of rest is a moment wasted. But reframing this mindset is crucial. Think of self-care like charging your phone - you simply can't help anyone when you're running on empty. I've learned over the years that the key to sustainable relaxation is keeping it simple, involving your family when possible, and focusing on progress rather than perfection.

Expect and plan for interruptions, and celebrate small wins along the way. Remember that missing a day of rest isn't failure - giving up entirely is. When you notice how differently you parent when rested versus exhausted, it becomes clear that taking time to recharge isn't selfish. It's essential maintenance for being the father your family deserves and needs.

THE FATHER YOU BECOME: HEALTH AS A FOUNDATION FOR STRONG FATHERHOOD

Let me share a comment I received from a dad in the chat section of Fathering Strong. "I used to think being strong meant never showing weakness. Now I realize true strength is taking care of myself so I can take care of others. My son told me yesterday, 'Dad, I want to be strong like you.' He wasn't talking about my muscles - he was talking about how I handle stress, how I make time for what matters, how I take care of myself and our family." His son understands what Fathering Strong really means.

When we talk about being a strong father, physical health strengthens four core virtues that are essential to fatherhood. First, health builds courage by giving you the energy to face daily challenges, the confidence to speak up about your needs without guilt, and the ability to show your kids that self-care takes bravery. It allows you to lead by example, even when it's difficult. Second, health develops fortitude by building the stamina to stay present through long days and developing resilience through consistent healthy habits. This teaches your children the value of persistence and allows you to show up fully, even during tough times. Third, health strengthens faith by helping you trust in the process of gradual improvement and believe in your ability to change and grow. It helps you model spiritual and physical wellness while understanding that health is a gift to be cherished. Finally, health deepens love by giving you the energy to fully engage with your family and create healthy traditions that bond you together. When you demonstrate self-love through healthy choices, you teach your children self-worth and build a legacy of wellness for future generations.

CREATING YOUR SUCCESS BLUE-PRINT WITH SMART HEALTH GOALS

The key to lasting change isn't setting huge goals - it's setting SMART ones (Specific, Measurable, Achievable, Relevant, Time-bound). Let me share some example goals with the intended results. Choose the ones that work best for you or make up your own.

Starting With Movement

> - Initial Goal: "I will do 5 push-ups every time I brush my teeth for the next month"
> - Result: Built up to 50 push-ups a day without disrupting family time
> - Key Learning: "The best exercise routine is the one you'll actually do"

Nutrition That Works

> - Initial Goal: "I will prep healthy snacks every Sunday for the upcoming school week"
> - Result: His daughter started asking for the "special daddy snacks"
> - Key Learning: "When I stopped forcing health food and started modeling it, everything changed"

Relaxation for Real Life

> - Initial Goal: "I will do 2 minutes of deep breathing during my daily commute"
> - Result: Found himself handling baby's 3 AM wake-ups with more patience
> - Key Learning: "Small moments of peace add up to big changes in parenting"

YOUR FIRST 30 DAYS

Here's an example of how to build your own path using SMART goals:

Week One: Choose Your Starter Goal

Pick ONE of these proven winners:

> ‣ Movement: "I will walk for 10 minutes during my lunch break, three times this week"
> ‣ Nutrition: "I will eat one serving of vegetables with dinner every day this week"
> ‣ Relaxation: "I will do three deep breaths before starting my car, every time"

Week Two: Add Family Connection

Build on your foundation:

> ‣ Movement: "We will have a 15-minute family dance party every Saturday morning"
> ‣ Nutrition: "We will try one new fruit or vegetable as a family each week"
> ‣ Relaxation: "We will start bedtime 10 minutes earlier for quiet family reading"

Weeks Three and Four: Create Your Routine

Strengthen your practice:

> ‣ Movement: "I will join my kids in active play for 20 minutes after work, three times per week"
> ‣ Nutrition: "We will cook one meal together as a family every Sunday"
> ‣ Relaxation: "I will start and end each day with a one-minute gratitude practice"

YOUR NEXT CHAPTER STARTS NOW

The journey to becoming a stronger, healthier father isn't about dramatic transformations - it's about small, consistent choices that add up over time. Start with one goal, celebrate small wins, and remember: every step forward, no matter how small, is progress your family will notice.

Let me end this chapter with a story that brings everything full circle. When I was running the Lifegevity Program I received a photo from Chris, a dad who was 40, overweight, and seeking to improve his overall health. The picture showed him teaching his son to ride a bike - something he couldn't do when he first joined the program because of his health. But that wasn't why he sent the photo. He sent it because of what his son said during that moment, "Dad, I'm not scared to try because you're strong enough to hold me up."

That's what this chapter is really about. Physical health isn't just about looking good or living longer - it's about being strong enough to hold up the ones we love, in all the ways they need us to.

Through our journey together in this chapter, we've discovered that true physical strength as a father means:

- Having the energy to be present when your family needs you
- Building healthy habits that your children will carry into their own lives
- Finding balance between taking care of yourself and caring for others
- Creating a foundation of wellness that strengthens your entire family

Remember this, start where you are, not where you think you should be. Small, consistent actions matter more than perfect plans. Your health choices are silent lessons for your children. Taking care of yourself isn't selfish - it's essential. And every step forward, no matter how small, counts. Your children don't need you to be perfect. They need you to be present, healthy, and strong enough to help them grow.

CHAPTER 9

SPIRITUAL HEALTH - CONNECTING WITH THE TRUE FATHER

Like many dads, I spent years focusing on what I thought mattered most - staying fit, managing my emotions, and providing financially for my family. These are all important, of course. But through my own journey of fatherhood, I've discovered something far more fundamental: the bedrock of being a great dad is your spiritual health. It reminds me of Jesus's powerful teaching in Matthew 7:24-27, where He compares the wise man who built his house on rock to the foolish one who built on sand. That's exactly what we're talking about here - building your fatherhood on the unshakeable foundation of a genuine connection with God.

Think about it: when your kids are struggling, when work gets overwhelming, or when you're facing tough decisions, where do you turn for strength? God designed us to find our strength in Him. As Psalm 46:1 reminds us, "God is our refuge and strength, an ever-present help in trouble." This isn't just religious talk - it's about developing a real, living relationship with your heavenly Father who guides your decisions and sustains you through life's challenges.

Building spiritual strength is like developing any important relationship - it takes time, attention, and genuine effort. When you invest in this connection with God, something amazing happens: you gain clarity about right and wrong, and you find the courage to choose what's right, even when it's hard. It's like wearing invisible armor (Ephesians 6:10-18) that protects your heart and mind, helping you face each day's challenges with renewed faith and unwavering hope.

PRACTICES FOR SPIRITUAL GROWTH

Just as Paul compared our spiritual journey to athletic training (1 Corinthians 9:24-27), building spiritual strength requires consistent practice. As I discussed in the previous chapter, you wouldn't expect to get physically fit by working out once a month, right? The same principle applies to your spiritual life.

To grow spiritually, you need to intentionally make time each day to pray, study the Bible, connect with fellow believers, and live out your faith through serving others. As James 1:22 reminds us, Do not merely listen to the word, and so deceive yourselves. Do what it says." Let me share some real stories of fathers who've experienced this transformation firsthand.

Take Mike, for example. He joined a Fathering Strong group for fathers with teenagers. Like many dads, he worried about fitting one more thing into his packed schedule. But what happened next amazed him. The wisdom he gained from studying Scripture with other fathers completely transformed how he handled family conflicts. Instead of raising his voice when his teenagers challenged him, he learned to listen first and respond with grace - modeling the patience our heavenly Father shows us.

Then there's Andy and his wife, who committed to praying together each evening after putting their kids to bed. They took seriously the biblical principle that "a cord of three strands is not quickly broken" (Ecclesiastes 4:12). While it felt awkward at first - and yes, sometimes they were too tired - their persistence paid off. Their unity in parenting grew stronger through shared prayer. When their son later faced anxiety, they tackled it as a team, offering both practical support and spiritual guidance rooted in God's promises.

Fred's story particularly inspired me. He chose to demonstrate his faith through action, taking Jesus's words in Matthew 25:40 to heart: "Whatever you did for one of the least of these brothers and sisters of mine, you did for me." Fred started taking his step-children to volunteer at their local food bank. This hands-on practice of living out God's love made a visible impact - his children began showing more compassion to their classmates, and their family bonds grew stronger through serving together.

These fathers discovered something powerful: investing in spiritual growth doesn't just change you - it transforms your entire family. Their children witnessed authentic faith in action, not just faith in words. Their homes became places where, as Joshua declared, "But as for me and my household, we will serve the LORD" (Joshua 24:15). The patience, understanding, and wisdom they gained through consistent spiritual practices rippled out to touch every aspect of their family life.

Spiritual growth isn't about perfection - it's about progress. Each small step you take to strengthen your spiritual life builds a stronger foundation for your family's faith journey. As you continue reading this chapter, we'll explore specific ways you can develop these practices in your own life, starting with the powerful tool of prayer.

PRAYER: YOUR DIRECT LINE TO GOD

Let me tell you something I've learned the hard way: prayer isn't just another item on your spiritual to-do list - it's your lifeline as a father. Jesus showed us this when He would regularly slip away to pray, even in His busiest moments (Luke 5:16). As fathers, we need this connection even more.

Think of prayer as your direct line to the perfect Father. Imagine having 24/7 access to the wisest, most loving dad who ever existed - that's exactly what prayer gives you. As Jeremiah 33:3 tells us, God says, "Call to me and I will answer you and tell you great and unsearchable things you do not know." What an incredible promise for us as fathers!

In my years of talking to other dads and working on my own prayer life, I've witnessed prayer work in countless ways. Sometimes it's a desperate cry for help when your teenager is rebelling, while other times it's a quiet moment of gratitude when your toddler finally drifts off to sleep. Every prayer matters to God, whether big or small.

Prayer isn't just about speaking - it's about stopping to listen to what the world is telling you. It's about tuning in to that voice in your head and truly paying attention to its message. Over the years, I've discovered that God wasn't silent at all; I just wasn't listening and responding. The conversation was always there, waiting for me to engage.

Here are the main types of prayer that can strengthen your role as a father:

- ➤ Praise: Start by acknowledging God's greatness - it puts your challenges in perspective
- ➤ Confession: Being honest with God about your mistakes models humility for your kids
- ➤ Thanksgiving: Cultivating gratitude changes how you view daily parenting challenges
- ➤ Asking: Yes, God wants to hear about your needs - even the small ones
- ➤ Praying for Others: This expands your heart and teaches your children to care for others
- ➤ Quiet Prayer: Sometimes, the most powerful prayer is just listening for God's guidance

BUILDING PRAYER INTO YOUR CHILDREN'S LIVES

As a Fathering Strong dad, you have the incredible privilege of helping your kids discover the power of prayer and build their own relationship with God. Let me share something personal - something I wish I had done differently when my kids were growing up. While we faithfully said grace at dinner, I never truly helped them develop their own prayer life. I prayed for them daily, but I made the mistake of thinking my silent prayers were enough.

Looking back now, with the wisdom that comes from both experience and God's Word, I see the missed opportunities. Deuteronomy 11:19 tells us to teach God's ways to our children, "talking about them when you sit at home and when you walk along the road, when you lie down and when you get up." I wish I had prayed with my daughter each night about her math struggles or helped my son seek God's peace before basketball tryouts. Those simple moments could have taught them what James 5:13 teaches: "Is anyone among you in trouble? Let them pray. Is anyone happy? Let them sing songs of praise."

We might have kept a prayer journal together, writing down how God showed up when they needed to make new friends or face difficult situations at school. Imagine how powerful it would have been to help my children create their own record of God's faithfulness. Through this practice, they could have learned to make prayer their first response to challenges rather than trying to handle everything on their own. I hope this book helps you make the moments with your children that I missed with mine.

Based on what I've learned over the years - both from Scripture and from engaging with other fathers - here are some practical ways to help your kids develop a meaningful prayer life:

Make Prayer a Daily Connection

> - Weave prayer naturally into your family's rhythm - during meals, bedtime, or a special family prayer time
> - Show your kids that prayer matters by making it as routine as brushing teeth

Remember Jesus's words about finding a quiet place to pray (Matthew 6:6) - help each child create their own special prayer spot

Explore Different Prayer Styles

- ➤ Help them discover various ways to pray - written prayers, spontaneous conversations with God, or even drawing their prayers
- ➤ Use the Psalms as examples of different ways to express ourselves to God
- ➤ Let them find what feels natural and meaningful to them, just as David danced before the Lord while others prayed quietly

Pray Aloud for Them

- ➤ Let them hear you bring their worries, dreams, and everyday moments to God
- ➤ Model the confidence of Philippians 4:6-7 , bringing everything to God in prayer
- ➤ When you pray about their math test or friendship struggles, they learn that nothing is too small for God's attention

Nurture Compassion Through Prayer

- ➤ Guide them in praying beyond themselves - for the new kid at school, a sick grandparent, or people affected by natural disasters
- ➤ Help them understand Jesus's command to "love your neighbor as yourself" through prayer
- ➤ Use prayer time to develop their hearts for others

Create a Prayer Adventure

- ➤ Start a simple prayer journal together, maybe with stickers or drawings for younger kids
- ➤ Celebrate when you see God's answers, even in unexpected ways
- ➤ Use Psalm 34:17 as encouragement: "The righteous cry out, and the LORD hears them"

Share Your Prayer Story

> Tell them about your own prayer journey - both the victories and the times you struggled to understand God's response
> Be honest about times when God's answers looked different than expected
> Help them understand that prayer is about relationship, not just requests

Keep it Age-Appropriate

> Talk about prayer in ways they can grasp
> With little ones, keep it simple ("God loves hearing from you!")
> As they grow, dive deeper into prayer's meaning and power, using Scripture as your guide

Live it Out

> Your example matters most - let them catch you praying during daily life before important decisions, in moments of gratitude, or when facing challenges
> Show them how to "pray continually" (1 Thessalonians 5:17)

When you make prayer a priority and guide your children in developing their own prayer life, you build a spiritual foundation that will anchor your family in God's truth. You're giving them a lasting gift - teaching them to turn to their heavenly Father in all circumstances. This is what being a Fathering Strong dad is all about: leading your children to develop their own authentic relationship with God through prayer.

THE POWER OF THE WORD: BIBLE STUDY AS A CORNERSTONE OF SPIRITUAL GROWTH

Remember when you first became a father? If you're like me, you probably wished babies came with instruction manuals. Well, here's the truth I've learned: God actually gave us the ultimate parenting guide - His Word. As 2 Timothy 3:16-17 tells us, "All Scripture is God-breathed and is useful for teaching, rebuking, correcting and training in righteousness, so that the servant of God may be thoroughly equipped for every good work." This includes being equipped for fatherhood.

Along with prayer, reading the Bible regularly is essential for every father's spiritual growth. It's not just about checking off a religious duty - it's about getting to know God's heart and His ways. Through Scripture, we discover who God is, what He wants for us, and the incredible promises He makes to us as fathers an our children.

During my own struggles with parenting, I've always found comfort and direction in Scripture. Let me share a personal example: When my son was going through a difficult time in middle school, I found myself turning to the Psalms for guidance. Reading about David's challenges and his unwavering faith gave me perspective on how to support my son through his struggles. The words weren't just ancient text anymore - they became a practical blueprint for navigating modern parenting challenges.

The Bible provides practical wisdom about:

> Marriage (Ephesians 5:25-33)
> Parenting (Ephesians 6:4)
> Managing finances (Proverbs 22:7)
> Building relationships (Romans 12:18)
> Making decisions (James 1:5)
> Handling conflict (Matthew 18:15-17)

To grow spiritually through Bible study, here are some approaches that have worked for me and other Fathering Strong dads:

Make it a Daily Priority

> Set aside a specific time (many dads find early morning works best)

> - Start with just 15 minutes - consistency matters more than length
> - Use the Fathering Strong 30-Day Devotional*(I will show you how to use this in Chapter 15)* as a starting point

Choose Your Study Method

> - Read through one book at a time (I recommend starting with John or Proverbs)
> - Follow a daily devotional guide
> - Listen to audio versions during your commute
> - Join a Bible study group or Fathering Strong community for accountability

Apply What You Learn

> - Keep a journal of insights specifically related to fatherhood *(I will explain this further in Chapter 15)*
> - Share what you're learning with your family
> - Look for ways to put God's Word into practice each day

In my experience, different Bible versions and study guides have served different purposes. The John Maxwell Leadership Bible (Maxwell 2007) helped me navigate work and family challenges. The Chronological Bible (Cargal, Chavalas and Edwards 2014) gave me a clearer understanding of the Biblical timeline and events. Find what works for you - the key is engaging with God's Word regularly.

Reading the Bible as a family creates special moments that your children will remember. Here's how to make it work:

> - Choose a consistent time (maybe during breakfast or before bed)
> - Keep it age-appropriate (use a children's Bible for younger kids)
> - Make it interactive (ask questions, act out stories)
> - Connect Scripture to daily life situations
> - Let your kids take turns reading as they get older
> - Pray together about what you've read

Looking back, I wish I had spent more time on spiritual connection when my children were growing up. While they attended Sunday school and participated in various church groups and youth outings, I now realize I missed valuable opportunities to build deeper relationships with them through shared prayer time. Actively engaging in prayer together could have created an even stronger family bond. It's a perspective that only comes with time and experience as a parent.

Bible reading isn't about accumulating knowledge - it's about transformation. As Hebrews 4:12 says, "For the word of God is alive and active." When you consistently engage with Scripture, you're not just strengthening your own faith - you're creating a legacy of biblical literacy and spiritual wisdom for your children.

Start small, but start today. Maybe begin with Proverbs - there's one chapter for each day of the month. Or read through a Gospel to understand Jesus's heart. The important thing is to make God's Word a central part of your life as a father.

During the COVID-19 pandemic, while quarantined at home, I found clarity about my life's direction through daily Bible reading. I randomly selected passages from the New Testament, and remarkably, each verse seemed to speak directly to what I needed to hear in that moment. It reminded me that sometimes you just have to put your trust in God's hands.

THE POWER OF COMMUNITY: CONNECTING WITH LIKE-MINDED FATHERS

Have you heard about the remarkable redwood tree? Despite towering hundreds of feet tall, its roots are surprisingly shallow. What keeps it standing through storms? Its roots interlock with other redwoods, creating an underground support network. That's exactly what fathers need - to be connected, supporting each other, standing stronger together than we ever could alone. That's exactly what Proverbs 27:17 means when it says, "As iron sharpens iron, so one person sharpens another." While personal spiritual practices like prayer and Bible study are crucial, God never intended us to walk this fatherhood journey alone.

I learned this lesson the hard way. For years, I tried to be the "lone ranger" dad, convinced I could figure everything out by myself. But time taught me an important truth: we simply can't be the best fathers by going it alone. Things changed when I joined a local fathers' group. There, I found men who truly understood my daily struggles, celebrated my parenting wins, and gently guided me back to God's truth whenever I felt lost. Their support transformed my journey as a father.

I witnessed the impact of supporting a father during his separation from his wife. Around the time the movie "Fireproof" (Cameron 2008) was released, I learned about the 40-day Love Dare challenge (Kendrick 2013). After sharing this resource with a close friend, he used its principles to reconnect with his wife, ultimately leading to their reconciliation. Their relationship has flourished over the years, thanks to the strong foundation they rebuilt through this process.

Being a father is one of life's greatest challenges, and trying to navigate it alone can leave you feeling overwhelmed and isolated. God designed us for community - to learn from each other, support one another, and grow together in faith. When fathers connect with other like-minded dads, they create a powerful support system that strengthens their ability to lead their families well. Here's why connecting with other dads matters.

Shared Understanding

> Other fathers face the same daily joys and struggles you do
> As Ecclesiastes 4:9-10 reminds us, "Two are better than one... If either of them falls down, one can help the other up"
> Your challenges aren't unique - other dads get it

Biblical Encouragement

> - Hebrews 10:24-25 instructs us to "spur one another on toward love and good deeds"
> - Other dads can lift you up during tough times with Scripture-based wisdom
> - Together, you can celebrate God's faithfulness in your parenting journey

Genuine Accountability

> - Regular meetups create natural accountability for your spiritual goals
> - James 5:16 calls us to "confess your sins to each other and pray for each other"
> - Other fathers can lovingly call you back when you stray from God's path

Wisdom Transfer

> - Titus 2 emphasizes the importance of older men teaching younger ones
> - Experienced dads offer valuable insights from their own parenting journey
> - You can learn from both others' successes and mistakes

Kingdom Impact

> - When fathers support each other, entire families benefit
> - Your community strengthens as godly fathers lead their homes
> - Future generations are impacted by the legacy you build together

There is a local organization call "The Gathering" that is guided by these truths and brings men together. Their slogan resonates the purpose, "Connecting men to men and men to God."

THE FATHERING STRONG APP: YOUR CONNECTION POINT

As mentioned earlier, I developed the Fathering Strong app alongside Pastor Eli Williams and Urban Light Ministries. We designed it to help you build essential connections with other fathers. Think of it as your digital fellowship hall - a welcoming space where dads can gather, share experiences, and grow together in their parenting journey. Here's how to make the most of your experience.

Connect Authentically

- ▸ Join forums and chat groups focused on fatherhood and faith
- ▸ Message fathers who share your specific parenting challenges

Share Your Journey

- ▸ Be honest about your parenting struggles
- ▸ Share how God is working in your family
- ▸ Celebrate victories and support others in difficult times

Access Growth Resources

- ▸ Dive into articles and videos about faith-based parenting
- ▸ Share insights from your own Bible study and prayer time
- ▸ Learn from other fathers' experiences and wisdom

Join Local Activities

- ▸ Find face-to-face events in your area
- ▸ Connect with fathers in your local community
- ▸ Turn online connections into real-world friendships

Acts 2:42, describes the early church: "They devoted themselves to the apostles' teaching and to fellowship, to the breaking of bread and to prayer." This same pattern works for fathers today. When you regularly meet with other dads to discuss life's important matters, share both struggles and victories, and pray together, you're following God's design for spiritual growth.

I've seen it happen countless times: a dad joins a Fathering Strong community feeling overwhelmed and isolated, but through consistent connection with other fathers, he finds strength, wisdom, and encouragement. One father recently told me, "I thought I was the only one struggling with my teenager's attitude. But in our group, I found hope and practical biblical solutions from dads who'd been there."

The Fathering Strong app offers an ideal starting point, but don't stop there. Look for opportunities to connect with fathers at your church, in your neighborhood, or through your children's activities. As Galatians 6:2 instructs us to "carry each other's burdens," these connections become lifelines during challenging seasons of fatherhood.

Going it alone as a dad can leave you exhausted and discouraged. But when you connect with other fathers who share your commitment to spiritual growth, you'll find the support, wisdom, and fellowship God designed us to need. This isn't just about friendship - it's about building a brotherhood of fathers who encourage each other to lead their families in God's ways.

PUTTING FAITH INTO ACTION: LIVING OUT YOUR BELIEFS

James 2:17 tells us that "faith by itself, if it is not accompanied by action, is dead." This truth hit home for me one Sunday after church when my son asked, "Dad, why do we only talk about helping people but never actually do it?" His innocent question exposed a gap between what I said I believed and how I lived. Maybe you've experienced something similar?

Your faith isn't just about praying and reading the Bible - it's about living out what you believe in ways your children can see, touch, and experience. When Jesus said, "Let your light shine before others, that they may see your good deeds and glorify your Father in heaven" (Matthew 5:16), He was calling us to active, visible faith.

Let me share my personal journey. During my early working years, I compartmentalized my faith to Sundays and failed to connect it with my parenting. Work deadlines and activities consumed my time. While I provided for my family and maintained discipline, something felt incomplete. Have you ever felt that disconnect?

The transformation began when I started integrating my faith into daily life. Here's what changed:

> Established regular Bible study habits and journaled my reflections
> Deepened my church involvement by teaching parenting classes and other adult educational classes
> Started helping my wife on her passion to reach other mothers with Biblical truths and support through her website HappyHeartMinistries.com
> Made serving others a family priority

This transformation wasn't immediate, and looking back, I wish I had started sooner to better support my children's growth. Through this journey, I developed greater patience (Galatians 5:22-23), understanding, and wisdom. My anger triggers diminished as I learned to embrace the wisdom of being "quick to listen, slow to speak and slow to become angry" (James 1:19). I became more intentional about child-rearing, viewing my parental role through God's eyes. All of this helped as I continue to grow as a father and now grandfather.

Most importantly, I began seeing my children as God's unique creations. Psalm 139:14 took on new meaning as I celebrated their individual gifts, walked alongside them through challenges, and guided them with God's wisdom rather than relying solely on my own understanding.

MAKING SERVICE A FAMILY VALUE

When you help others, something beautiful happens - you shift focus away from yourself toward meeting others' needs. This naturally cultivates empathy and humility, drawing us closer to God's heart. Jesus modeled this servant leadership when He washed His disciples' feet (John 13:14-15), showing us how to lead our families through service.

Children learn primarily through observation. When they see their father actively serving others and giving his time, they witness authentic Christianity in action. This hands-on demonstration becomes more powerful than any sermon or lesson. As 1 John 3:18 reminds us, "Let us not love with words or speech but with actions and in truth."

PRACTICAL WAYS TO PUT FAITH INTO ACTION

Here are a few examples on how to involve your family in serving others and build a lasting legacy of compassion. These time-tested methods will help create meaningful experiences while making a real difference in your community:

Food Bank Ministry

- ➤ Sort donations or pack food boxes together
- ➤ Use this time to discuss Jesus's teachings about feeding the hungry
- ➤ Let kids experience the joy of directly helping families in need

Church Service

- ➤ Serve as a family in children's ministry
- ➤ Help with setup/cleanup for events or do the offering take up during services as a family
- ➤ Welcome new families together

Neighbor Outreach

- Help elderly neighbors with yard work
- Organize a neighborhood cleanup
- Prepare meals for families during difficult times

Community Impact

- Participate in local homeless outreach or Habitat for Humanity building project
- Join environmental cleanup efforts
- Support school supply drives

Global Awareness

- Sponsor a child as a family
- Pack Christmas boxes through Operation Shoebox
- Support missionary families through letters and care packages

Daily Kindness

- Help someone with groceries
- Write encouraging notes to others
- Share meals with those who are lonely

Hospital/Nursing Home Visits

- Bring joy to those who are sick or lonely
- Make cards and small gifts
- Read to residents or play music

Remember to process these experiences with your children. Ask questions like:

- "How did helping others make you feel?"
- "Where did you see God working today?"
- "What did you learn about Jesus through serving?"

When fathers unite in service, we create a powerful force for positive change in our communities. The father-absent epidemic affecting so many neighborhoods can only be addressed when godly men step up and model Christ-like service not only to their own families but to others who lack father figures. By serving alongside other dads and their families, we build networks of support, mentorship, and accountability. These connections strengthen the fabric of our communities and provide living examples of God's design for fatherhood. As your family serves others, you'll likely encounter children and teens who need positive male role models. Your consistent presence and service can help fill this void, creating ripple effects that extend far beyond your immediate family. Remember, strong fathers build strong families, and strong families unite to build strong communities that reflect God's love and grace.

THE IMPACT OF ACTIVE FAITH

When you put your faith into action and involve your kids in helping others, you're not just strengthening your own faith - you're building a legacy. As Deuteronomy 6:6-7 instructs, you're teaching God's ways diligently to your children, showing them how faith works in real life.

Think of each act of service as a seed planted in your children's hearts. These seeds grow into:

- Compassion for others (Colossians 3:12)
- Understanding of God's love (1 John 4:19)
- Recognition of their own blessings (2 Corinthians 9:11)
- Desire to make a difference (Matthew 25:40)

Start small, but start today. Choose one way your family can serve others this week. As you consistently put your faith into action, you'll watch your children grow in their understanding of God's love and their role in His kingdom work.

SMART GOAL SETTING FOR SPIRITUAL GROWTH

As we wrap up this chapter, let's talk about turning these spiritual principles into practical action. Proverbs 21:5 tells us, "The plans of the diligent lead to profit as surely as haste leads to poverty." This applies to our spiritual growth too. Setting SMART goals can help you develop the spiritual disciplines we've discussed.

Let me share how SMART goals transformed my own spiritual journey. When I first started, my goals were vague: "pray more" or "read the Bible sometimes." Nothing changed until I got specific and started setting goals like "pray with each child for 5 minutes before bedtime" and "read one Proverb every morning before work."

Here are practical SMART goals that have worked for fathers in our Fathering Strong community.

Prayer Goals

- ➤ Basic Level:
  - "I will pray each morning from 6:00-6:10 AM, following the ACTS method (Adoration, Confession, Thanksgiving, Supplication), starting tomorrow for 30 days"
  - "I will pray with each of my children for 5 minutes at bedtime, focusing on their specific needs and concerns, every night this week"
- ➤ Advanced Level:
  - "I will maintain a prayer journal, writing down requests and answers daily, reviewing it weekly with my spouse for the next three months"
  - "I will organize and lead a weekly family prayer time every Sunday evening from 7:00-7:30 PM, including praise, thanksgiving, and family needs"

Bible Study Goals

- Basic Level:
  - "I will read one chapter of Proverbs daily during my lunch break, writing down one parenting insight to apply that day"
  - "I will complete one Fathering Strong devotional each morning before work, spending 15 minutes in reflection"
- Advanced Level:
  - "I will study the book of Ephesians every day over the next six weeks, focusing on Paul's teaching about family relationships"
  - "I will memorize one Scripture verse about fatherhood each week, reviewing it with my children during dinner time"

Community Connection Goals

- Basic Level:
  - "I will attend the men's group at church twice monthly for the next three months, sharing at least one parenting challenge each session"
  - "I will connect with two other dads through the Fathering Strong app each week, engaging in meaningful conversations about faith and fatherhood"
- Advanced Level:
  - "I will form a weekly prayer partnership with another father, meeting every Tuesday at 6:30 AM for the next six months"
- "I will organize a monthly fathers' breakfast group at my home, inviting 5-7 dads for fellowship and prayer"

Service and Faith-in-Action Goals

- Basic Level:
  - "My children and I will serve at the food bank on the first Saturday of each month from 9:00-11:00 AM for the next six months"

- "Our family will help elderly neighbor Mrs. Johnson with yard work one Saturday morning each month, showing God's love through practical service"
- Advanced Level:
  - "I will lead my family in adopting a missionary family, communicating monthly and meeting their practical needs for one year"
  - "We will organize a quarterly community service project, involving at least three other families each time"

Remember, spiritual growth isn't about perfection—it's about progress. As Philippians 1:6 assures us, "He who began a good work in you will carry it on to completion until the day of Christ Jesus." Each small step you take builds a stronger foundation for your family's faith journey.

Start today by choosing one goal. Write it down, share it with someone who will hold you accountable, and take that first step. As you grow stronger spiritually, you'll find yourself becoming more and more the father God designed you to be, leading your family with wisdom, courage, and grace.

Remember, "With God all things are possible" (Matthew 19:26). You've got this! And, more importantly, God's got you.

CHAPTER 10

EMOTIONAL WEALTH - MASTERING YOUR INNER WORLD

When most people think about wealth, they picture money in the bank. I've met countless fathers in our Fathering Strong community who believed a bigger bank account would solve their problems. But as Scripture reminds us in Matthew 6:21, "For where your treasure is, there your heart will be also." Experience shows that money alone rarely brings lasting happiness or fulfillment in our role as fathers.

As we explored in the last chapter, spiritual well-being gives you the foundation to be a good father. Now, we'll examine another crucial element of strong fatherhood that God designed: building your emotional wealth. Think of it as developing the "fruit of the Spirit is love, joy, peace, forbearance, kindness, goodness, faithfulness, gentleness, and self-control." (Galatians 5:22-23).

Your emotions guide how you connect with others, form relationships, and experience life. Emotional wealth - having a rich inner life, understanding others' feelings, and creating meaningful connections - contributes far more to fulfillment than financial success. Even vast material wealth feels hollow without emotional intelligence and healthy relationships. As King Solomon, the wisest and wealthiest man of his time, wrote in Proverbs 4:23, "Above all else, guard your heart, for everything you do flows from it."

The Lifegevity program we discussed in earlier chapters places significant emphasis on emotional well-being as a cornerstone of holistic health. Research (Stapleton, Stress Management - A Guaranteed Approach for Maximizing Your Health 2009) consistently shows that emotional health directly impacts physical health, relationship quality, and overall life satisfaction. When fathers prioritize their emotional well-being, they're better equipped to handle life's challenges and create lasting bonds with their families.

This chapter focuses on understanding and managing your inner world through four essential areas: emotional regulation, stress management, vulnerability, and healthy communication. We'll explore these vital emotional skills, from regulating feelings and handling stress to practicing vulnerability and communicating effectively. Through my years of counseling fathers, I've seen how these skills transform families. True strength isn't about suppressing emotions or maintaining a tough facade - it's about understanding your feelings and expressing them in ways that honor God and serve your family.

EMOTIONAL REGULATION: THE KEY TO EMOTIONAL WEALTH

As I grow older and build deeper connections with fellow fathers, I often share this profound truth: emotional regulation isn't just a modern psychological concept - it's a biblical principle that God intentionally wove into the fabric of strong fatherhood. Scripture repeatedly addresses how we should manage our emotions, particularly in James 1:19: "Be quick to listen, slow to speak and slow to become angry." This divine wisdom perfectly captures the essence of emotional regulation: understanding our feelings, recognizing our triggers, and consciously choosing our responses rather than reacting on impulse.

Let me tell you about Steve, a father who struggled with anger during his kids' bedtime routine. "I'd lose my cool every night," he admitted during a dad's discussion group. "Then I started practicing what we learned about emotional regulation - pausing, praying, and choosing my response. Now bedtime has become a precious time of connection with my children." Steve's story shows how emotional regulation creates the peaceful home environment described in Proverbs 15:1: "A gentle answer turns away wrath, but a harsh word stirs up anger."

When you master emotional regulation, you're better equipped to:

- Create a Christ-centered atmosphere of peace in your home
- Model God's patience and grace for your children
- Handle conflicts with wisdom rather than reaction
- Build stronger bonds with your spouse and kids
- Teach your children healthy ways to manage their own emotions

Remember David in the Bible? Despite being a mighty warrior, he wrote psalms expressing his full range of emotions - from joy to anger to fear - while ultimately submitting them to God's control. That's emotional regulation at its finest.

I've seen this transformation countless times in our community. Take Michael, an emergency room doctor who brought his workplace stress home every night. Through practicing self-control and implementing specific emotional regulation techniques, he learned to transition from work mode to father mode. "I now pray in my car before entering the house," he shared. "It helps me leave the hospital stress behind and be fully present with my family."

Here are some practical ways to better regulate your emotions while staying grounded in faith:

PRACTICE THE PRAY METHOD

- Pause (Step back from the situation)
- Reflect (Consider what God's Word says)
- Ask (Seek God's wisdom in the moment)
- Yield (Choose a response that honors Him)

Recognize Physical Signs

▸ Notice how your emotions show up in your body
▸ Pay attention to triggers that challenge your peace
▸ Use these awareness moments as prayer prompts

Apply Deep Breathing

▸ Take slow, deep breaths while meditating on Scripture
▸ Remember God's command to "be still and know that I am God" (Psalm 46:10)
▸ Use this time to reset your emotional state

Take Spirit-Led Breaks

▸ Step away when emotions run high
▸ Use this time for quick prayer or Bible verse meditation
▸ Return to the situation with renewed perspective

Transform Your Thoughts

▸ Replace negative thoughts with biblical truth
▸ Challenge assumptions with God's promises
▸ Focus on "whatever is true, whatever is noble..." (Philippians 4:8)

James found these strategies transformative during his teenage son's rebellious phase. "Instead of responding with anger, I learned to pause and pray," he shared. "This changed everything. My son saw that Dad wasn't just preaching self-control - I was living it."

Remember, emotional regulation isn't about suppressing feelings - it's about managing them in a way that reflects God's character. When you regulate your emotions well, you're not just building emotional wealth - you're creating a legacy of spiritual and emotional health for your children.

For many fathers, this journey begins with small steps. Start today by choosing one situation where you typically react strongly. Apply these principles and watch how God transforms that challenge into an opportunity for growth and connection with your family.

STRESS MANAGEMENT: FINDING PEACE WHEN LIFE GETS BUSY

Life can feel overwhelming for dads juggling work, family, and daily responsibilities. I see it every day in our Fathering Strong community - fathers trying to balance it all while carrying the weight of providing, protecting, and leading their families. But here's what I want you to remember: even Jesus took time to step away and find peace when life got busy (Mark 6:31). Managing stress isn't just about survival; it's about following God's design for balanced, healthy fatherhood.

The Lifegevity program, which was discussed in Chapter 8, aligns beautifully with biblical principles of rest and renewal. Just as God established a rhythm of work and rest in creation, we need to establish healthy patterns to manage our stress. When you learn to handle life's pressures effectively, you'll experience the peace that Jesus promised - not as the world gives, but His perfect peace that transcends understanding (John 14:27).

Let me share Thomas's story. As a small business owner and father of four, he was constantly stressed about making ends meet. "I was worried and upset about many things, but missing what was really important." Through applying stress management principles and practical Lifegevity relaxation techniques, he found a new way of living. "Now I start each day with God, and that sets the tone for everything else."

Here are proven stress management techniques that combine biblical wisdom with practical application:

SPIRIT-LED MINDFULNESS

> Start with Scripture meditation
> Focus on God's promises when anxiety rises
> Practice being present in each moment

Deep Breathing:

> Use deep breaths to slow down, inhale God's peace, and exhale your stress
> Remember that God's Spirit gives life and peace (Romans 8:6)
> Take pauses throughout your day and concentrate specifically on your breathing

Purposeful Movement

> Exercise as a form of renewal and connection
> Walk and pray, following Jesus' example of active solitude
> Use physical activity to burn off stress while connecting with God

Sacred Time Management

> Schedule regular rest
> Create boundaries that honor God and family
> Practice saying "no" to preserve your peace
> Remember: "There is a time for everything" (Ecclesiastes 3:1)

Healthy Self-care

> Honor God through self-care habits
> Establish regular sleep patterns
> Choose nourishing foods and limit stress-inducing substances
> Remember your body is a gift to be stewarded

Connect with Nature

> ➤ Use nature as a reminder of God's faithfulness
> ➤ Find restoration in quiet outdoor spaces

Mark is a father who transformed his family's life by applying these principles. As a high-powered executive, he used to wear his stress like a badge of honor. "I thought being stressed meant I was working hard enough," he shared. "But my kids were getting my leftovers." Mark learned to start his day with prayer and Scripture instead of emails. He began taking short walks during lunch to pray and reflect. "My stress didn't disappear," he says, "but I learned to carry it differently, with God's help."

The research behind the Lifegevity program confirms what Scripture has always taught: when we manage stress God's way, we experience better physical and spiritual health. Participants in the Lifegevity program who implemented these stress management techniques reported:

> ➤ Improved sleep quality
> ➤ Better relationships with their children
> ➤ More patience in parenting
> ➤ Stronger marriages
> ➤ Enhanced work performance
> ➤ Deeper spiritual connections

Jesus said, "Come to me, all you who are weary and burdened, and I will give you rest" (Matthew 11:28). Managing stress isn't just about techniques - it's about trusting God's promises and following His design for balanced living. When you learn to rest in Him while applying these practical tools, you'll become the steady, peace-filled father your family needs.

Start today by choosing one area where stress typically overwhelms you. Apply these principles and Lifegevity techniques, then watch how God transforms your response to pressure into an opportunity for peace and spiritual growth.

VULNERABILITY: BEING OPEN WITH OTHERS

Being vulnerable means opening up about your feelings, fears, and uncertainties. For many fathers, this feels like walking into uncharted territory. Society tells us that men need to be tough and stoic - that showing emotion somehow makes us less masculine. But God's Word paints a different picture. Throughout Scripture, we see great leaders being vulnerable: David poured out his heart in the Psalms, Paul admitted his weaknesses (2 Corinthians 12:9-10), and even Jesus shared his struggles with his closest disciples in Gethsemane.

Here's the truth: real strength isn't about hiding your feelings - it's about facing them with God's help. Being vulnerable takes more courage than maintaining a tough facade. When you show your kids that even Dad makes mistakes and feels uncertain sometimes, you're teaching them powerful lessons about grace and authenticity, and it's okay not to be perfect.

Think about it like a two-way street. When you're honest about your feelings with your spouse and kids, they're more likely to share their own struggles with you. Your openness creates a safe space for everyone. When children see their dad talking about his emotions, they learn that their feelings are valid too. This shapes how they'll handle relationships throughout their lives.

Vulnerability isn't weakness - it's one of the bravest things you can do. In a world that constantly tells men to "toughen up" and hide their emotions, it takes real courage to share your true feelings. When you open up and let others see the real you, that's what creates deep, lasting bonds with the people who matter most in your life.

As challenging as it is, maintaining courage and fortitude remains essential when facing the discomfort of being vulnerable. Many fathers have discovered their lives transformed in unexpected ways after taking this brave step. Here are a few examples of dads who dove into the pool of vulnerability.

James's Breakthrough

James struggled to connect with his teenage son until he started sharing stories about his own adolescent challenges. "I told him about my failures, my fears, even my faith struggles," James shared. "That's when everything changed. Now my son comes to me for advice about things I never dreamed he would."

Michael's Journey

As a corporate executive, Michael always hid his work stress, thinking it protected his family. Following the example of Paul's openness about his trials, Michael began sharing appropriately about his challenges. "My kids saw that it's okay to not have everything figured out," he says. "Now we pray together about our struggles."

Peter's Transformation

Peter learned to pause and pray instead of yelling when frustrated with his young children. His seven-year-old daughter caught on quickly. During one stressful moment, she reminded him, "Daddy, remember what you taught us - we can tell God anything." His vulnerability had taught her about honest communication with both family and God.

Let's explore some practical ways to cultivate vulnerability in your daily life. When implemented consistently, these approaches can transform your relationships with both your family and God. Here are a few key practices to consider.

Share your feelings (in the right way): Don't dump adult problems on your kids, but share age-appropriate emotions they can relate to. For example, saying "I'm feeling nervous about my presentation today" helps them understand that everyone experiences anxiety sometimes.

Admit when you're wrong: Apologize sincerely when you make mistakes, like "I'm sorry I raised my voice earlier. That wasn't the right way to handle things." This shows your kids that taking responsibility is a strength, not a weakness.

Share your worries (in a healthy way): Open up to your spouse or close friends about your concerns. Try saying something like "I could use your perspective on this challenge I'm facing."

Ask for help: Remember that seeking support shows wisdom, not weakness. Whether it's asking for advice or an extra hand with daily tasks, it's okay to lean on others.

Listen with care: When family members share their feelings, give them your full attention. Avoid interrupting or judging - just listen and validate their emotions with responses like "That sounds really tough" or "I hear you."

When you lean into your core virtues of courage, fortitude, faith, and love, showing vulnerability becomes an act of strength rather than weakness. Your courage gives you the power to face your fears about opening up, while fortitude helps you persist even when being vulnerable feels uncomfortable. Faith reminds you that showing your authentic self aligns with your deeper values and purpose as a father. And perhaps most importantly, love - for your family and yourself - provides the motivation to create deeper connections through emotional honesty. These virtues work together, giving you the inner resources to overcome any hesitation about being vulnerable with your loved ones. When you embrace vulnerability from this place of strength, you create profound teaching moments for your children and forge unshakeable bonds within your family.

HEALTHY COMMUNICATION: BUILDING STRONG FAMILY RELATIONSHIPS

Good communication isn't just a skill—it's a biblical principle woven throughout Scripture. From God's intimate conversations with Adam in the garden to Jesus's compassionate dialogues with His disciples, we see that meaningful communication builds stronger relationships. In our Fathering Strong community, we've witnessed how fathers who master communication principles create homes where every family member feels heard, understood, and valued.

Learning to speak up for yourself while remaining respectful is a crucial skill. This means expressing your thoughts and feelings honestly and clearly, while still considering others' perspectives. The goal is to strike a balance - avoid being too passive and letting others dominate, but also steer clear of aggressive or controlling behavior.

The Lifegevity program identified that being assertive and expressing yourself reduces stress levels (Stapleton, Lifegevity Wellness Program 2001). Effective communication gives you better problem-solving tools and a greater sense of control, leading to decreased anxiety and worry. When you communicate clearly and confidently, you're more likely to have your needs met and maintain healthier relationships with others. The program's research showed that people who practiced assertive communication techniques experienced lower blood pressure, better sleep quality, and improved immune system function. Additionally, those who learned to express their thoughts and feelings in a direct, honest way reported higher levels of self-esteem and more satisfying personal and professional relationships. This positive impact on mental health creates a ripple effect, enhancing overall well-being and quality of life.

When you communicate well, you strengthen trust in your relationships and create a more harmonious home environment. Expressing your thoughts and feelings respectfully boosts your self-esteem and confidence, helping you feel more secure in who you are.

Good communication prevents minor issues from escalating into major conflicts, reducing stress for the entire family. Remember that children learn communication skills by observing their parents. By modeling effective communication, you're equipping them with valuable life skills they'll carry into adulthood.

Fathers who learned to communicate more effectively found greater joy and success in their lives. Here are examples of fathers who experienced this improvement.

Tom, a construction worker and single dad, struggled to connect with his teenage daughter. "I used to just give quick answers," he admitted. After learning to listen actively and ask thoughtful questions, everything changed. "Now, my daughter and I have real conversations about life, faith, and her future. She even discovered my passion for architecture, which became our special connection point."

Steve, who coaches Little League, realized he was too focused on results rather than understanding his son's feelings about sports. When he started asking questions like "How did you feel about the game?" instead of analyzing performance, his son's confidence grew. Now they enjoy sports together, and his son actively seeks his advice about other life challenges too.

These fathers found that better communication didn't just improve their relationships - it made parenting more enjoyable and rewarding. They report feeling more connected to their families and experiencing less stress in their daily lives.

WAYS YOU CAN IMPROVE YOUR COMMUNICATIONS

The Bible provides clear principles for healthy communication that we can apply in practical ways. It starts with listening before speaking, as James 1:19 teaches. This means giving others your complete attention, observing both words and body language, and asking questions to ensure understanding.

Following Ephesians 4:15, we must speak truth with love. This involves using "I" statements to express feelings, sharing concerns respectfully, and finding the balance between honesty and kindness. When we follow Proverbs 15:1's guidance to guard our words, we choose language that builds up rather than tears down. We must think before speaking and consider how our tone affects others.

Creating safe spaces for communication means establishing regular family discussion times and making room for different viewpoints. When others show vulnerability, we respond with acceptance and maintain appropriate confidentiality. Finally, we must practice forgiveness by addressing conflicts promptly, apologizing sincerely, and modeling reconciliation for our children.

Remember, "The tongue has the power of life and death" (Proverbs 18:21). Your words can either build bridges or create barriers in your family relationships. Choose to communicate in ways that reflect God's character—with patience, kindness, and understanding.

The impact of improved communication extends beyond your immediate family. As you model these skills, you're teaching your children how to build healthy relationships in their own lives. You're also creating a legacy of open, honest, and grace-filled communication that can influence generations to come.

Start today by choosing one communication principle to focus on this week. Perhaps begin with active listening or speaking words of encouragement. Ask God for wisdom and guidance as you practice these skills.

CREATING SMART GOALS FOR EMOTIONAL WEALTH

Just as we're called to be intentional in our spiritual growth, we need to be purposeful in developing our emotional wealth. SMART goals give us a framework to begin building our emotional wealth and turn biblical principles into daily practices. Let's look at specific goals for each area:

Emotional Regulation

> - Practice deep breathing exercises for 5 minutes each morning before the kids wake up for the next 30 days
> - Keep a daily emotion journal for 2 weeks, noting triggers and responses to stressful situations
> - Set aside 10 minutes each evening to reflect on emotional reactions of the day and plan better responses

Stress Management

> - Schedule two 15-minute breaks during workdays for the next month to step away and reset
> - Establish a weekly "worry time" - 30 minutes each Sunday to address concerns and plan solutions
> - Exercise for 20 minutes three times per week to reduce stress levels

Showing Vulnerability

> - Share one personal challenge or learning experience with your children each week
> - Have a monthly "feelings check-in" with each family member individually
> - Write one letter per month to your children expressing your hopes, fears, and love for them

Healthy Communication

> - Practice active listening without interrupting during family dinner conversations five times per week
> - Schedule 15-minute one-on-one talks with each child twice per week
> - Replace criticism with "I feel" statements three times per day when addressing concerns

BUILDING YOUR EMOTIONAL WEALTH
AND THE IMPACT ON FATHERHOOD

As Proverbs 16:32 reminds us, "Better a patient person than a warrior, one with self-control than one who takes a city." Building emotional wealth transforms your journey as a father by drawing on the core virtues of strong fatherhood. It takes real courage to face your emotions honestly and commit to personal growth. Your fortitude helps you persist through the challenging work of developing emotional intelligence and resilience. Faith gives you confidence that investing in your emotional health will create lasting benefits for your family. And love - both for yourself and your family - forms the foundation for all emotional growth and connection.

When you invest in building emotional wealth, you become better equipped to handle life's challenges with grace and wisdom. This inner strength enables you to create the stable, nurturing environment your children need to thrive. By modeling emotional intelligence and self-care, you teach your children powerful lessons about personal growth and healthy relationships.

Remember that caring for your emotional well-being isn't selfish - it's essential to be the father your family deserves. Through courage, fortitude, faith, and love, you build the emotional resources needed to guide your family through life's journey. This investment in yourself creates a powerful legacy that shapes not just your children's lives but generations to come. That's the true essence of Fathering Strong.

CHAPTER 11

FINANCIAL WISDOM: STEWARDING GOD'S RESOURCES AS A FATHER

As we continue our journey in becoming stronger fathers, let's tackle a challenge that many of us face daily: managing money. In Matthew 6:24, Jesus teaches us that "No one can serve two masters... You cannot serve both God and money." This profound truth sets the foundation for our discussion about finances - not from the world's perspective of accumulation but from God's perspective of stewardship.

I remember sitting at my kitchen table late one night, surrounded by bills and feeling overwhelmed by financial pressure. In that moment of desperation, I turned to my Bible for guidance and found Philippians 4:19: "And my God will meet all your needs according to the riches of his glory in Christ Jesus." This powerful verse changed everything about how I viewed money management. It helped me realize that true financial wisdom isn't just about budgets and spreadsheets - it's about trusting in God's faithful provision while doing our part as responsible stewards of what He's given us.

BIBLICAL PRINCIPLES OF FINANCIAL STEWARDSHIP

The Bible offers us more than 2,000 verses about money and possessions - more than it says about faith and prayer combined. This emphasis shows us how important proper financial management is in our spiritual lives.

Let's look at five key areas that will help us become better stewards of what God has entrusted to us.

Creating a Budget

Proverbs 21:5 tells us, "The plans of the diligent lead to profit as surely as haste leads to poverty." A budget is simply a plan for your money that helps you honor God with your resources. When you understand where every dollar goes you can make smarter spending choices, find opportunities to save, and ensure you are living within your means. A clear budget puts you in control of your financial future.

Saving Wisely

"The wise store up choice food and olive oil, but fools gulp theirs down" (Proverbs 21:20). God's Word encourages prudent saving while warning against hoarding. Whether you're preparing for unexpected expenses or working toward major life goals like homeownership or your children's education, consistent saving makes it possible. Even small amounts - like $20 per week - can grow into significant savings over time.

Investing for the Future

The Parable of the Talents (Matthew 25:14-30) teaches us about the importance of growing what God has given us. Think of investing as putting your money to work for you. By placing funds in stocks, bonds, or real estate, you give your money the potential to grow over the long term. While investing offers opportunities for growth, it's wise to consult a financial advisor who can help you understand the risks and choose investments that match your goals.

Managing Debt

"The borrower is slave to the lender" (Proverbs 22:7). This powerful warning reminds us to be very careful with debt. Debt can feel like a heavy weight that limits your financial freedom. Smart debt management starts with understanding your loans, maintaining timely payments, and avoiding unnecessary borrowing. Focus first on paying off high-interest debt - it's often the biggest drain on your finances.

Generous Living

"God loves a cheerful giver" (2 Corinthians 9:7). Our giving reflects God's generous character. Financial stewardship means handling money responsibly. This includes making thoughtful spending decisions, helping others when possible, and avoiding waste. Remember that money is a tool - use it wisely to benefit both yourself and others in your community.

REAL STORIES OF GOD'S PROVISION

When fathers put these practices in place, they found their lives to be less stressful and more joyful. Taking control of your finances requires faith, courage, and fortitude, along with trust that God will provide for your needs. Here are a few examples of how fathers improved their parenting by mastering their finances.

A few years ago, I met Tom, a father of three who was struggling with mounting credit card debt. During a discussion with other fathers he learned about Luke 14:28 "Suppose one of you wants to build a tower. Won't you first sit down and estimate the cost to see if you have enough money to complete it?" This verse inspired Tom to create his first real budget. Within 18 months, he eliminated $15,000 in debt and began saving for his children's education.

James, faced a different challenge. Despite a good income, his family constantly argued about money. During counseling, their pastor directed them to Ecclesiastes 5:10 "Whoever loves money never has enough." This truth helped James and his wife realize they were chasing material wealth at the expense of their family's peace. They began holding weekly budget meetings, praying together about financial decisions, and teaching their children biblical money principles.

CREATING A GOD-CENTERED BUDGET

When King David prepared to build the temple, he said, "But who am I, and who are my people, that we should be able to give as generously as this? Everything comes from you, and we have given you only what comes from your hand" (1 Chronicles 29:14). This humble acknowledgment that everything belongs to God should guide our budgeting process.

A budget is your foundation for financial strength. It's more than tracking expenses - it's creating a roadmap for your money that aligns with your family's values and priorities. A well-planned budget reduces money stress and helps you take better care of your family both today and tomorrow.

This financial stability creates a sense of security for everyone. With a clear budget, you can confidently save for important milestones like homeownership, your children's education, and retirement. Watching your progress toward these goals keeps you motivated and focused.

Financial stress often strains relationships, but a solid budget puts you in control and fosters a more peaceful home environment. You can also use budgeting as a teaching tool, explaining money concepts to your kids in age-appropriate ways and modeling responsible financial habits. These valuable life skills will serve them well into adulthood.

Let me share how Mark, a father in our community, transformed his family's finances through biblical budgeting. "I used to see budgeting as restrictive," he told me, "but Proverbs 27:23 changed my perspective: 'Be sure you know the condition of your flocks, give careful attention to your herds.'" Mark realized that just as a shepherd needs to actively manage his flock, he needed to actively manage his finances. He started with these practical steps, which I encourage you to follow:

STEPS TO CREATE YOUR FAMILY BUDGET

Start with Prayer

Before touching any numbers, pray for wisdom. James 1:5 promises, "If any of you lacks wisdom, you should ask God, who gives generously to all without finding fault."

Calculate Your Income

List all sources of income, remembering Paul's words in 1 Timothy 6:17 not to "put your hope in wealth, which is so uncertain, but to put your hope in God."

Track Your Spending

For one month, record every expense. This might feel tedious, but Proverbs 14:8 reminds us that "the wisdom of the prudent is to give thought to their ways."

Prioritize Giving

Make giving your first budget item. "Honor the Lord with your wealth, with the first fruits of all your crops" (Proverbs 3:9). Many Christian families start with a tithe (10%) and add other giving as God provides.

Plan Essential Expenses:

Next, budget for needs like housing, food, and utilities. Remember Jesus' teaching about prioritizing necessities (Matthew 6:31-33).

Include Savings:

"The wise store up choice food and olive oil" (Proverbs 21:20). Set aside money for emergencies and future needs.

Plan Discretionary Spending:

With remaining funds, budget for wants while being mindful of contentment. As Paul wrote, "I have learned to be content whatever the circumstances" (Philippians 4:11).

PRACTICAL TOOLS FOR BUDGETING

While the Bible provides our principles, modern tools can help us apply them effectively. Consider these proven methods and tools.

The 50/30/20 rule (Whiteside 2024) provides a biblical framework for balanced stewardship: 50% for needs (essential living expenses), 30% for wants (discretionary spending), and 20% for savings and giving. This aligns with principles of wise resource management while ensuring margin for both saving and generous giving.

Zero-based budgeting (Kagan 2024), where every dollar is assigned a purpose before the month begins, reflects the biblical principle of intentional stewardship. As Proverbs 27:23 teaches us to "be sure you know the condition of your flocks," this method helps us account for every resource God provides.

The envelope system (Lake 2025), whether physical or digital, brings powerful accountability to spending. Some fathers have found success using various envelope approaches to manage their finances. Some prefer traditional physical envelopes for tracking variable expenses like groceries and entertainment, while others embrace digital envelope systems through apps for managing fixed monthly bills. Many have discovered that a hybrid approach, combining both physical and digital methods, offers the most comprehensive solution for their family's needs.

Today's technology offers powerful tools to help implement these budgeting methods. Here are several trusted digital solutions that can strengthen your family's financial stewardship:

- YNAB (You Need A Budget): Excellent for zero-based budgeting with strong educational resources (ynab.com)
- Mint: Free option with good expense tracking and bill management (mint.intuit.com)
- Goodbudget: Digital envelope system that works well for families (goodbudget.com)
- Personal Capital: Strong for investment tracking alongside budgeting (personalcapital.com)

TEACHING CHILDREN THROUGH BUDGETING

Your budget becomes a powerful teaching tool for your children. My daughter learned about delayed gratification when she was determined to buy a car for her final year of high school. She wanted to drive herself to school, so she learned to budget her spending to save enough money carefully. Through this experience, she discovered the value of managing her finances and the satisfaction of working toward a long-term goal.

Remember, a God-centered budget isn't about restriction - it's about freedom to serve God and your family without financial stress. When challenges arise, return to Matthew 6:33: "But seek first his kingdom and his righteousness, and all these things will be given to you as well." Let this verse guide your financial decisions, reminding you that budgeting is ultimately about aligning your resources with God's purposes for your family.

SAVING AND INVESTING: BUILDING YOUR FAMILY'S FINANCIAL FUTURE

As a father, one of your greatest responsibilities is ensuring your family's financial security through wise saving and investing. I learned this lesson deeply when my daughter was born, realizing that every dollar saved today could mean greater opportunities for her future. Whether it's funding her education, handling unexpected medical expenses, or having resources to help others in need, the importance of building a strong financial foundation through consistent saving and prudent investing cannot be overstated.

The Bible reminds us that "The wise store up choice food and olive oil, but fools gulp theirs down" (Proverbs 21:20). This principle of saving and investing isn't just about accumulating wealth - it's about being prepared to care for our families and bless others. When we save wisely and invest carefully, we're better positioned to respond to both the challenges and opportunities God places in our path.

Think of saving as building your family's financial foundation. Just as Noah prepared for the flood by building the ark, we prepare for life's storms through consistent saving. Whether it's an unexpected car repair or a temporary job loss, savings provide the security your family needs. Beyond emergencies, saving helps you achieve important goals like buying a home, funding your children's education, or preparing for retirement.

Investing takes saving a step further by putting your money to work. The Parable of the Talents (Matthew 25:14-30) teaches us about growing what God entrusts to us. Through wise investing, even modest amounts can grow significantly over time through the power of compound interest.

Here's a practical approach to saving and investing that has helped many fathers.

- Start with Prayer: Ask God for wisdom in managing His resources
- Build Your Emergency Fund: Set aside 3-6 months of expenses in an easily accessible account
- Set Clear Goals: Define what you're saving for and when you'll need the money
- Create a Savings Plan: Begin with what you can, even if it's just $25 per month
- Learn About Investing: Understand basic investment options like stocks, bonds, and mutual funds

- ▸ Start Early: Remember, time is your greatest advantage with investing
- ▸ Diversify Wisely: Don't put all your eggs in one basket
- ▸ Seek Godly Counsel: Consider working with a Christian financial advisor

To help you get started, here are some useful tools:

- ▸ Savings Apps: Acorns rounds up your purchases and saves the difference (acorns.com)
- ▸ Investment Platforms: Betterment (betterment.com) and Wealthfront (wealthfront.com) offer automated investing
- ▸ Traditional Brokers: Fidelity, Schwab, and Vanguard provide comprehensive services
- ▸ Educational Resources: Crown Financial Ministries (crown.org) offers biblical investment guidance

Remember, saving and investing isn't about hoarding wealth - it's about stewarding God's resources wisely to care for your family and bless others. As you build your financial future, keep Proverbs 13:22 in mind: "A good person leaves an inheritance for their children's children." Through faithful saving and investing, you're creating a legacy that can impact generations.

STEWARDSHIP: MANAGING MONEY WITH PURPOSE

While budgeting, saving, and investing form essential financial habits, stewardship should be the guiding principle behind all money decisions. As 1 Peter 4:10 teaches us, "Each of you should use whatever gift you have received to serve others, as faithful stewards of God's grace in its various forms." Stewardship means recognizing that God owns everything and has entrusted us with resources to manage wisely - not just for our benefit, but for His purposes. This perspective transforms how we view money, shifting our focus from accumulation to faithful management of what God has provided.

Scripture consistently teaches that we're called to be good stewards of all God provides. When you embrace this truth, it naturally leads to more thoughtful decisions about saving, spending, and giving. Rather than chasing short-term satisfaction, you'll find yourself considering the eternal impact of your financial choices.

Good stewardship inherently involves generosity and caring for others. When your children see you sharing resources and helping those in need, they learn powerful lessons about responsibility and compassion. These experiences shape them into thoughtful stewards who understand money's potential to advance God's kingdom.

Living with a stewardship mindset brings remarkable peace. Instead of anxiety about finances or constant pursuit of material goods, you'll experience greater contentment and freedom from money worries.

STEWARDSHIP PAYS HIGH DIVIDENDS FOR FATHERS

Stewardship requires setting clear goals and taking action with courage, fortitude, and faith. Consider these inspiring examples of fathers who committed to faithful stewardship and witnessed God's faithfulness:

Peter, a father of four, felt God calling him to increase his giving despite uncertainty after a job change. He and his wife stepped out in faith, committing to tithe 10% even when it seemed impossible. Within months, God provided an unexpected promotion that not only covered their increased giving but enabled them to start their children's college fund. Even more meaningful, Peter's example profoundly influenced his teenage sons, who began managing their allowances with greater wisdom and generosity.

Andy and his wife made the courageous choice to live on 70% of their income, saving 20% and giving away 10%, while still paying their mortgage. This required significant lifestyle adjustments and trust in God's provision. Their careful budgeting and intentional spending united the family as they made financial decisions together. Their children learned valuable lessons about delayed gratification and generosity, and they found joy in supporting missionaries and helping families in need. An unexpected blessing came when Andy could retire early, allowing him to mentor young fathers in financial stewardship and family leadership.

When we trust God and manage finances according to His principles, we open ourselves to His blessings - not just materially, but in the lasting impact we have on our children and others. Good stewardship isn't about accumulating wealth; it's about faithfully managing what God has given us and teaching our children to do the same. As these stories demonstrate, when we align our financial decisions with biblical principles, we create a legacy of faith, wisdom, and generosity that extends far beyond our bank accounts.

Managing money well demonstrates your faith in action. You're not just teaching your kids good habits; you're building a family that understands wise financial stewardship. This forms a crucial part of being a strong father and making a lasting difference in your family and community.

BREAKING FREE FROM THE BONDAGE OF DEBT

"The rich rule over the poor, and the borrower is slave to the lender" (Proverbs 22:7). These sobering words from Scripture capture a truth I learned the hard way. When I started my business, I needed to purchase equipment and office furniture. The lending companies would only approve the purchases and provide loans if I agreed to be personally liable for the debt. Eager to get my business off the ground, I accepted their terms without fully understanding the risks.

This decision came back to haunt me when another company purchased the building where my business was located, forcing me to close operations. The burden of those personal guarantees fell squarely on my shoulders, creating a financial strain that I'm still managing today. Looking back, I see how that biblical wisdom about debt and borrowing played out in my own life and how a better, more guided understanding, may have changed my decision and my life.

UNDERSTANDING DEBT FROM GOD'S PERSPECTIVE

The Bible doesn't completely forbid debt, but it consistently warns us about its dangers. Consider these principles.

Debt Creates Bondage: "Do not be one who shakes hands in pledge or puts up security for debts" (Proverbs 22:26).

Paying Debts is Required: "The wicked borrow and do not repay, but the righteous give generously" (Psalm 37:21).

Wisdom Prevents Debt: "The prudent see danger and take refuge, but the simple keep going and pay the penalty" (Proverbs 27:12).

REAL STORIES OF DEBT FREEDOM

Mike's story powerfully illustrates the journey to financial freedom. As a father of three, he had racked up $43,000 in consumer debt through what he described as "living carelessly." After studying Scripture's teachings about debt, he and his wife made bold changes to their lifestyle. They sold their new car and purchased a reliable used one, downsized to a smaller home, launched a side business, and eliminated their credit cards. Mike shared that the most challenging aspect was explaining to their children why certain activities were no longer affordable. However, this led to meaningful conversations about contentment and trusting in God's provision. Their dedication paid off - within three years, they had eliminated all debt except their mortgage, and their children had gained invaluable lessons about financial responsibility.

PRACTICAL STEPS TO DEBT FREEDOM

Breaking free from debt requires a systematic approach grounded in biblical wisdom and practical action. As a father, you can implement clear, actionable steps to achieve financial freedom. Start by stopping all new debt - cut up or freeze your credit cards, delete stored payment information from online shops, and commit to using only cash or debit cards.

Next, get clear on your numbers. List every debt with its balance and interest rate, track all spending, and create a realistic repayment plan. Two biblical approaches have proven particularly effective: the Snowball Method (Kamel 2024) and the Avalanche Method (Egan 2021). With the Snowball Method, you pay minimum payments on all debts while putting extra money toward your smallest debt, building momentum through quick wins. The Avalanche Method targets your highest-interest debt first, saving more money long-term but requiring more discipline.

While paying off debt, start building an emergency fund with $1,000. Once you're debt-free, grow this fund to cover 3-6 months of expenses. This financial buffer prevents you from falling back into debt when unexpected costs hit, like car repairs or medical bills. Think of it as a shield protecting your family's financial future.

DEALING WITH COMMON DEBT CHALLENGES

Let's examine how three fathers successfully navigated different types of debt challenges while maintaining their commitment to biblical financial principles.

Student Loans

Alex, a young father in our church, faced the daunting challenge of $80,000 in student loans. Through careful planning and dedication, he created a sustainable approach by living on a strict budget and utilizing income-based repayment options. He also strategically applied any extra income directly to the principal and eventually found employment with a company that offered student loan repayment benefits as part of their compensation package.

Medical Debt

When Tom's son needed unexpected surgery, the resulting medical bills threatened to overwhelm his family's finances. He took proactive steps by immediately negotiating with the hospital's billing department and establishing a reasonable payment plan. By requesting financial assistance and maintaining open communication with his creditors, Tom was able to manage the debt while continuing to meet his family's other needs.

Mortgage Debt

Peter and his wife approached their mortgage with biblical wisdom, implementing several key principles that kept their housing costs manageable. They committed to keeping their mortgage payment under 25% of their monthly income and made extra principal payments whenever possible. They also resisted the temptation to refinance for consumer purchases or upgrade to a larger home unnecessarily, focusing instead on being content and building equity in their current home.

TEACHING CHILDREN ABOUT DEBT

Teaching children about debt requires tailoring the message to their developmental stage while laying a foundation for lifelong financial wisdom.

For young children, focus on basic concepts they can grasp through everyday experiences. Use their toys to demonstrate borrowing and returning, emphasizing the importance of keeping promises. Help them understand delayed gratification by creating simple saving goals for desired items. Start them on the path to good financial habits by providing a piggy bank and celebrating when they save instead of spend.

With teenagers, dive deeper into real-world financial challenges they'll soon face. Have frank discussions about the dangers of credit card debt, showing them how interest compounds and small purchases can balloon into significant debt. Walk them through the actual costs of college education, exploring different funding options and their long-term implications. Include them in family conversations about debt-free goals, helping them understand how financial decisions impact the entire family's future.

WHEN DEBT FEELS OVERWHELMING

When the weight of debt feels crushing, remember that God hasn't abandoned you. This journey requires courage to face your financial reality, fortitude to persist through challenges, faith in God's promises, and love for your family that motivates lasting change.

Draw courage from Joshua 1:9, "Be strong and courageous. Do not be afraid; do not be discouraged, for the Lord your God will be with you wherever you go." Let fortitude grow through Romans 5:3-4: "We also glory in our sufferings, because we know that suffering produces perseverance; perseverance, character; and character, hope."

Your faith remains anchored in God's promise from Philippians 4:19 that "my God will meet all your needs according to the riches of his glory in Christ Jesus." While working through debt challenges, seek wisdom from godly counselors, remembering that "Plans fail for lack of counsel, but with many advisers, they succeed" (Proverbs 15:22).

Let love for your family fuel your determination, knowing that "It always protects, always trusts, always hopes, always perseveres" (1 Corinthians 13:7). Take encouragement from Zechariah 4:10, which reminds us to "not despise these small beginnings, for the Lord rejoices to see the work begin." Each step toward financial freedom, no matter how small, matters in God's eyes and to the legacy you leave for your family.

Remember, becoming debt-free isn't just about financial freedom - it's about being free to serve God without the bondage of financial stress. Your journey to debt freedom may take time, but each step brings you closer to the peace and opportunity that comes with financial freedom. Start today, even if it's just listing your debts or making one extra payment. Your family's future is worth the effort.

FINANCIAL SMART GOALS THROUGH A BIBLICAL LENS

Here are examples of SMART goals to strengthen your family's finances and build lasting security. These specific, measurable, achievable, relevant, and time-bound objectives will guide your household toward better money management and financial stability:

Budgeting Goals

> - **90-Day Budget Mastery** - Create and maintain a written monthly budget for three consecutive months, tracking every dollar spent and adjusting categories as needed until your budget accurately reflects your family's needs and priorities.
> - **Six-Month Spending Reset** - Reduce non-essential spending by 15% over six months, redirecting saved money toward giving and saving goals while teaching your family contentment with less.

Saving Goals

> - **Quick-Start Emergency Fund** - Build initial $1,000 emergency fund within three months through consistent weekly savings deposits, creating protection against unexpected expenses.
> - **Family Security Fund** - Establish 3-6 months of living expenses in emergency savings within one year through automated monthly savings of 15% of income.

Investing Goals

- **Retirement Kickstart** - Begin retirement contributions within three months at the minimum percentage needed to receive full employer match, ensuring long-term family provision.
- **Diversification Plan** - Create a balanced investment portfolio across 3-4 asset classes within one year, working with a financial advisor to match investments with your family's goals and risk tolerance.

Stewardship Goals

- **Faithful Giving Plan** - Establish consistent tithing of 10% gross income within three months, honoring God with your first fruits and teaching children about generous giving.
- **Kingdom Impact Fund** - Build a separate giving fund within six months by saving 5% beyond tithe, creating resources for helping others as God directs.

Debt Management Goals

- **Credit Freedom Plan** - Eliminate all credit card debt within six months using the snowball method, focusing intense effort on the smallest balances first while maintaining minimum payments on other debts.
- Debt Liberation Strategy - Clear all consumer debt except mortgage within two years through a systematic debt snowball approach, creating financial freedom for increased giving and saving.

Remember Proverbs 21:5, "The plans of the diligent lead to profit, as surely as haste leads to poverty." Choose the goals that best fit your situation, write them down, and review them regularly with your family.

BUILDING PROSPERITY THROUGH
WISDOM AND STEWARDSHIP

As fathers, we carry a profound responsibility that extends far beyond earning an income. Managing our family's finances with wisdom and purpose requires us to embody the essential virtues of courage, fortitude, faith, and love. It takes courage to face financial challenges head-on and make difficult changes to our spending habits. Fortitude helps us persist through the daily discipline of budgeting, saving, and eliminating debt. Faith reminds us to trust in God's provision while doing our part as diligent stewards. And love motivates us to make sacrifices today that will secure our family's tomorrow.

When we embrace these virtues in our financial lives, we create stability and security that allows our families to thrive. Our children learn invaluable lessons about responsibility, delayed gratification, and generosity by watching us manage money with purpose and wisdom. While material wealth isn't life's ultimate goal, being faithful stewards of our resources honors God and serves our families' needs both now and in the future.

This vital aspect of Fathering Strong challenges us to rise above society's consumer mentality and instead build true prosperity - one grounded in wisdom, stewardship, and eternal values rather than temporary possessions.

CHAPTER 12

A STRONG MARRIAGE:
THE FOUNDATION OF THE FAMILY

Picture James sitting at his kitchen table late one night, head in his hands, wondering how to repair his struggling marriage. Like many fathers, he knew his relationship with his wife affected their children, but he wasn't sure where to start. "My kids deserve better," he thought, "but how do I build the marriage they need to see?"

A strong marriage forms the foundation of a healthy family. When parents maintain a loving relationship, they create a stable and nurturing environment where children flourish. Think of Mike and Jenny, whose teenage daughter recently told them, "I know what real love looks like because I see it every day between you two." Their story, like many others you'll read in this chapter, shows how a strong marriage impacts the entire family.

Scripture provides clear direction for marriage, emphasizing love, unity, and mutual respect. The Bible shows us what a good marriage looks like through several key ideas, each illustrated by real fathers who've walked this path.

Unity in Marriage

When Alex left his parents' home to marry Lisa, he worried about balancing his old family with his new one. Genesis 2:24 spoke directly to his situation: "That is why a man leaves his father and mother and is united to his wife, and they become one flesh." John shares, "This verse helped me understand that creating our own family unit wasn't betraying my parents – it was following God's design."

The Power of Love

Carlos struggled with anger management until he encountered 1 Corinthians 13:4-7 in a men's group: "Love is patient, love is kind. It does not envy, it does not boast, it is not proud. It does not dishonor others, it is not self-seeking, it is not easily angered, it keeps no record of wrongs..." He recalls, "I started checking my behavior against this list every night. Was I patient with Maria today? Kind? It transformed how I treated her, and our kids noticed the difference."

Mutual Respect

"I used to think being the 'head of the household' meant making all the decisions," admits Robert. Then he studied 1 Peter 3, which instructs husbands to "be considerate as you live with your wives, and treat them with respect." Robert's perspective shifted: "Now I see that leadership means serving my wife and considering her wisdom in every decision. Our home feels completely different."

Selfless Partnership

Mike and Jenny's marriage changed when they truly understood Ephesians 5:21-33. "We stopped keeping score," Mike explains. "When the passage says to submit to one another 'out of reverence for Christ,' it clicked for us. I started asking myself, 'How can I serve Jenny today?' instead of waiting for her to serve me. Our kids saw us becoming true partners."

Lifelong Commitment

Peter and Sarah faced a crisis in their fifteenth year of marriage. Matthew 19:6 became their anchor: "So they are no longer two, but one flesh. Therefore what God has joined together, let no one separate." Peter shares, "We printed this verse and put it on our mirror. It reminded us daily that divorce wasn't an option – we had to work through our problems. That commitment gave our kids security during a tough time."

Even if you're not married to or living with your child's mother, maintaining a strong, respectful relationship with her is essential for your child's well-being. Take Stan's story: After his divorce, he made a conscious decision to never speak negatively about his ex-wife. "It was hard sometimes," he admits, "but I knew my daughters needed both of us working together. Now, five years later, we've built a respectful co-parenting relationship that put our daughters first."

Your child sees and loves both of you as their parents. When you work together and treat each other with respect, you help your child grow into an emotionally healthy and socially confident person. This means keeping your promises, following the agreed-upon schedule, and making key decisions about your child's life as a team. By putting your child's needs first and avoiding unnecessary conflict, you create a positive co-parenting environment where your child can thrive.

WHY A STRONG MARRIAGE MATTERS FOR BEING A BETTER FATHER

A happy, healthy marriage creates a strong foundation for the entire family. Mike, a father of three, learned this firsthand: "When Jenny and I worked on our relationship, our whole house felt different. The kids argued less, laughed more, and seemed more secure. I realized they were following our lead."

Children are like emotional sponges, absorbing everything they see at home. Tony, a family counselor and father, shares what he's observed both professionally and personally: "Kids don't just watch TV – they watch their parents. Every time you show respect to your wife, every moment you handle conflict with patience, you're teaching your children what love looks like."

When parents maintain a peaceful relationship, their home becomes a sanctuary of stability and safety. This environment allows children to develop confidence and emotional security. The strength of your marriage directly impacts your children's well-being.

This chapter will show you practical ways to build a stronger marriage. You'll learn how to communicate better, show love meaningfully, handle disagreements wisely, and work together toward common goals. By investing in your marriage, you create a more stable home for your children and become a more effective father.

GOOD COMMUNICATION MAKES YOUR RELATIONSHIP STRONG

Peter remembers the moment he realized his communication style was hurting his marriage. "I was always interrupting my wife Sarah, trying to fix everything instead of just listening," he admits. "Then our pastor pointed me to James 1:19 'Everyone should be quick to listen, slow to speak and slow to become angry.' That verse changed everything about how I communicate with Sarah."

Good communication forms the bedrock of a strong marriage. It's more than just talking – it's creating a safe space where both spouses can share their deepest thoughts, feelings, and dreams. When you master this skill, you follow the wisdom of Proverbs 18:21, "The tongue has the power of life and death." Your words can either build up your marriage or slowly tear it down.

Consider Peter's transformation: "I used to bottle everything up, thinking I was keeping the peace. Then I learned about Ephesians 4:15, speaking the truth in love. Sarah and I started having 'heart talks' every evening after the kids went to bed. Just 15 minutes of honest, loving conversation has brought us closer than we've been in years. Our teenage daughter even noticed, saying 'You and Mom seem happier lately.'"

Here's what effective marriage communication looks like in practice:

> **Give Full Attention:** Put away your phone, make eye contact, and show you're engaged through your body language
> **Listen to Understand:** Focus on truly hearing your spouse instead of planning your response
> **Use "I" Statements:** Share feelings without blame ("I feel overlooked" rather than "You never listen")
> **Stay Respectful:** Even in disagreements, maintain a tone of respect and avoid harsh words
> **Check Understanding:** Reflect back what you heard to ensure you're on the same page

COMMUNICATION ISSUES FOR DADS WHO LIVE OUTSIDE THE HOME

For fathers living apart from their children's mother, communication takes on even greater importance. Stan, a divorced father of two, shares: "I learned to treat every interaction with my ex-wife as a business meeting – professional, focused on the kids, and emotion-free. It wasn't easy, but remembering Colossians 4:6 – 'Let your conversation be always full of grace' – helped me stay focused on what mattered: our children's well-being."

Here are examples to consider if you are co-parenting from separate homes:

> **Schedule Regular Check-Ins:** Set a specific day and time each week to talk with the child's mother about parenting updates, schedules, and concerns. For example, "I will call every Sunday at 7 PM to discuss our child's week."
> **Practice Active Listening:** Focus on listening without interrupting during conversations with the child's mother. For instance, "I will pause and summarize what she says before responding during our talks."

- **Use Positive and Respectful Language:** Commit to communicating in a calm and respectful tone, even during challenging discussions. For example, "I will use solutions-focused language in 90% of our conversations over the next month."
- **Share Updates Promptly:** Keep each other informed about important information regarding your child. For example, "I will notify her within 24 hours of any changes to my schedule or plans involving our child."

Strong communication skills strengthen your co-parenting relationship and create a healthier environment for your children. Even when living apart, effective communication remains an essential part of being a good parent.

INTIMACY BRINGS YOU CLOSER TOGETHER

"I thought intimacy just meant physical closeness," reflects James, a father of two, "until our marriage counselor helped us understand it's about connecting heart, mind, and spirit." Like many fathers, James discovered that true marital intimacy encompasses multiple dimensions that strengthen both marriage and family.

Think of intimacy as building bridges between hearts. As Solomon writes in Song of Solomon 8:6, "Place me like a seal over your heart, like a seal on your arm; for love is as strong as death." This beautiful imagery reminds us that deep marital connection requires intentional nurturing in four key areas:

Physical Intimacy: Expressing Love Through Touch

Physical connection in marriage goes beyond sexual intimacy to include simple acts of affection that strengthen your bond. Mark and Julie made a commitment to hug for 20 seconds each morning. "It felt long at first," Mark admits, "but now it's our daily reset button. That moment of connection sets the tone for our whole day."

Emotional Intimacy: Creating Safe Harbors

Andy and Connie transformed their marriage by creating what they call their "judgment-free zone" – daily time where they share feelings, dreams, and fears openly. "When Connie told me she felt scared about our son's health challenges," Andy shares, "instead of jumping to solutions, I just held her hand and listened. That moment brought us closer than any date night could."

Spiritual Intimacy: Growing Together in Faith

Peter and Sarah made a commitment to pray together every morning. "It felt awkward at first," Sarah admits, "but now it's the foundation of our relationship. By keeping God at the center of their marriage, they've created a spiritual backbone for their family.

Mental Intimacy: Sharing Life's Journey

"My wife and I were living parallel lives," recalls Mark. "We managed the house and kids together, but we weren't sharing our inner worlds." They started what they call "curiosity conversations" – discussing articles, books, or podcasts that interested them. "Now our dinner table is filled with real discussions, and our kids are learning to think deeply too."

PRACTICE POINTS FOR BUILDING INTIMACY

Here are key ways to strengthen the bonds of intimacy in your marriage.

> Create daily connection rituals that anchor your relationship. This might include sharing three gratitudes before bed, praying together in the morning, or taking a 10-minute walk after dinner. These small but consistent moments help maintain your emotional connection throughout busy days.
> Deepen your emotional bond through intentional practices. Make time for active listening without trying to "fix" problems, share one hope and one fear each week, and express specific

appreciation daily. These practices create the emotional safety needed for true intimacy to flourish.

▸ Strengthen your spiritual connection as a couple. Set aside time to read a Bible verse together each morning, attend worship services as a couple, and discuss how God is working in your lives. This spiritual foundation helps unite you in your values and life purpose.

▸ Build mental connection through shared learning and growth. Take time to share interesting articles or podcasts with each other, take an online course together, or have regular discussions about your goals and dreams. These activities keep your relationship intellectually stimulating and forward-moving.

A strong marriage needs intimacy to thrive. When you invest time in meaningful conversations, create shared experiences, and open your heart to your spouse, you build a relationship that can handle whatever life throws at you. This deep connection doesn't just make your marriage better – it creates a loving environment where your children can grow and learn what healthy relationships look like. While building intimacy takes consistent effort, the reward is a marriage filled with understanding, trust, and lasting love.

SHARED VALUES: YOUR FAMILY'S GUIDING COMPASS

"We were like two ships passing in the night," recalls Peter, "until we sat down and really talked about what matters most to us." He and his wife Sarah discovered what many couples learn: shared values act as a compass, guiding family decisions and shaping children's character.

Consider Joshua's ancient declaration in Joshua 24:15, "But as for me and my household, we will serve the Lord." Like Joshua, today's fathers must intentionally choose and champion their family's core values. Every decision we make either reinforces or undermines what we say we believe. Our kids are watching!

When families actively live out their values, they create a powerful legacy of purpose and meaning. Here's how real families put their values into action:

Faith in Daily Life

The Martinez family starts each morning with a simple prayer and Bible verse. "It's not elaborate," explains Carlos, "but it shows our kids that faith isn't just for Sundays." They live out Deuteronomy 6:7: "Impress them on your children. Talk about them when you sit at home and when you walk along the road."

Family Unity in Action

When Phil's family faced a major career decision, they turned it into a lesson about priorities. "We gathered everyone, even our youngest, to discuss moving for my job," shares Phil. "We asked ourselves: 'Does this align with our value of putting family relationships first?' Our kids saw us choosing family over financial gain."

PRACTICAL WAYS TO ALIGN YOUR VALUES

Living out your family's values requires intentional action and consistent practice. Here are three essential approaches that successful families use to keep their values at the center of daily life.

The first step is **defining your core values** together as a couple. Schedule what some families call a "values summit" with your spouse where you can write down your top 5 non-negotiable principles. Create simple statements explaining each value that everyone can understand. The Thompson family, for instance, created this statement on integrity: "In our home, we tell the truth, even when it's hard."

The second key approach is **making your values visible** in everyday life. Consider displaying your family values creatively in your home and creating regular rhythms that reinforce them. Celebrate moments when family members live out these principles. Alex, a father of two, shares how they do this: "We have 'Integrity Stars' on our fridge. When someone chooses truth over convenience, they get to put up a star."

The third crucial element is **handling value conflicts** wisely when they arise. Address differences respectfully with your spouse and use conflicts as teaching moments for your children. Show them how to prioritize competing values when situations aren't black and white. As Peter shares: "When our values of honesty and kindness seemed to conflict, we taught our kids that being truthful doesn't mean being unkind."

LIVING YOUR VALUES IN CHALLENGING TIMES

Andy and Connie faced this test early in their marriage when their business struggled. "We had always taught our kids about trusting God and maintaining integrity," Andy explains. "During the financial crisis, they watched us choose honesty over quick profits through dishonest business practices. It cost us in the short term but taught them priceless lessons about living what we believe."

For separated parents, shared values become especially crucial. Stephan and his ex-wife agreed on core principles for raising their children: "Even though we live apart, our kids know certain values – like respect, responsibility, and faith – are constant in both homes."

CREATING YOUR FAMILY LEGACY

Think of values as your family's spiritual inheritance. Proverbs 13:22 says, "A good person leaves an inheritance for their children's children." Jim, a grandfather now, sees this playing out: "The values my wife and I established in our marriage are now showing up in how our grown children parent their kids. It's like watching ripples spread across generations."

Here a some action steps you can take this week:

> Set aside one hour with your spouse to list and discuss your core values
> Choose one value to intentionally model this week
> Create a simple way to celebrate when family members demonstrate your values
> Start a "values journal" to record how your family lives out its principles

Remember, your kids don't need a perfect family; they need parents who consistently point them toward what matters most. When you and your spouse align on core values, you create a stable foundation that helps your children navigate life's challenges with confidence and clarity.

QUALITY TIME, APPRECIATION, AND AFFECTION: KEEPING LOVE STRONG

When life gets busy with work and family, it's easy to forget to nurture your marriage. Simple acts like spending quality time together, expressing gratitude, and showing affection keep your relationship strong and vibrant.

Quality time means being fully present with your spouse - not just sharing physical space while scrolling through your phone. Make time for activities you both enjoy, whether that's cooking dinner together, taking evening walks, or exploring new adventures as a couple.

These meaningful moments together strengthen your emotional connection and deepen your understanding of each other. They prevent that lonely feeling that can creep into even good marriages. When you're truly present, you create natural opportunities for open conversation and show your spouse they're a priority in your life.

Making Moments Matter

Mike and Lisa transformed their evening routine after realizing they spent more time on their phones than with each other. "We started what we call 'sacred hour' after the kids' bedtime," Mike shares. "No phones, no TV – just us talking, praying, or simply being together. Our whole marriage changed."

The transition wasn't easy at first. "It felt pretty awkward initially. We didn't know where to start or what to talk about," Mike admits. "But we committed to this time, and slowly but surely, it became easier to communicate. Now it's something we look forward to at the end of each day."

Through this intentional time together, they discovered the truth of Proverbs 18:22, "He who finds a wife finds what is good and receives favor from the Lord."

PRACTICAL WAYS TO STRENGTHEN YOUR BOND

Here are key practices that successful couples use to keep their connection strong and vibrant.

Daily connection rituals form the foundation of a strong marriage

Share "high-low" moments at dinner, exchange three specific appreciations, or take 10 minutes to debrief about your day. As Peter notes: "Our kids actually remind us now: 'Dad, did you tell Mom your high-low today?'"

Weekly investment keeps your relationship growing and dynamic

Schedule regular date nights (even at home), take a weekend walk together, or plan and cook a meal as a couple. Sarah shares: "Our Thursday night cooking dates have become sacred time. Sometimes we just make sandwiches, but it's our time."

Monthly traditions help maintain perspective and alignment

Have a marriage check-in, try something new together, or revisit your shared goals. Alex reflects: "Monthly check-ins helped us catch small issues before they became big problems."

For fathers living separately from their children's mother, quality time takes different forms. Stephan maintains respectful communication through scheduled co-parenting check-ins, positive acknowledgment of her parenting strengths, and clear, kind communication about the children's needs.

Showing Appreciation and Affection

John learned the impact of consistent appreciation: "I started writing one thing I admired about my wife on a sticky note each morning. Our teenage son recently said, 'Dad, I want a marriage like yours someday.' Those notes were teaching him more than I realized."

You can begin to building a stronger relationship this week with these simple steps

> ➤ Identify your biggest time-waster and replace it with couple time
> ➤ Schedule three 15-minute connection points in your day
> ➤ Plan one weekly activity you both enjoy
> ➤ Create a gratitude ritual to share appreciation daily

Remember that a strong marriage provides the foundation for a happy family and models healthy relationships for your children. By investing in your marriage consistently, you create a loving home filled with joy, respect, and security.

SMART GOALS FOR A STRONG MARRIAGE AND RELATIONSHIP

Here are example SMART goals to strengthen your marriage in key areas.

Communication Goals:

> - Schedule 15 minutes of uninterrupted conversation with your spouse each evening after the kids are in bed
> - Practice active listening by repeating back what your spouse says during important discussions
> - Send one thoughtful text message each day expressing appreciation or support
> - For separated fathers: Set up a weekly co-parenting meeting to discuss children's needs calmly and professionally

Intimacy Goals

> - Plan one date night every two weeks without discussing kids or household tasks
> - Share three specific compliments with your spouse daily
> - Spend 5 minutes each morning and evening in physical connection (hugging, holding hands)
> - For separated fathers: Maintain appropriate boundaries while staying respectful in all interactions

Shared Values Goals

> - Have a monthly discussion about family goals and priorities
> - Attend religious services or community events together twice monthly
> - Create a shared budget and review it together weekly
> - For separated fathers: Align on core parenting values and consistently model them for children

Quality Time Goals

- Plan one new shared activity or hobby to try together each month
- Take a 15-minute walk together three times per week
- Cook one meal together weekly without distractions
- For separated fathers: Create special traditions for your parenting time that honor your relationship with children while respecting boundaries

HOW A STRONG MARRIAGE HELPS THE WHOLE FAMILY

A strong marriage forms the bedrock of effective fatherhood, creating an environment where virtues flourish and shape the next generation. As Psalm 128:3 beautifully describes, "Your wife will be like a fruitful vine within your house; your children will be like olive shoots around your table." This image captures the ripple effect of a healthy marriage.

When parents maintain a strong marriage, they create an environment where children naturally absorb healthy relationship patterns. Through their parents' example, children learn the essential elements of lasting love - respect, commitment, forgiveness, and faith. These daily lessons shape how they view relationships and influence their future choices.

A thriving marriage impacts every aspect of family life. Children in homes with strong marital relationships typically show greater emotional stability, better academic performance, and healthier social development. The virtues demonstrated in their parents' marriage become foundational building blocks for their own character development.

By prioritizing your marriage you fulfill a crucial aspect of fatherhood. Your commitment to building and maintaining a strong marriage creates a legacy that can influence generations, embodying the principles of Fathering Strong in a powerful and lasting way.

CHAPTER 13

BUILDING LASTING BONDS
WITH YOUR CHILDREN

Let me share something personal with you. Looking back at my journey as a father, one of my biggest regrets is not understanding sooner just how crucial it is to build deep, loving relationships with your children. I spent so many years caught up in being the provider - making sure there was food on the table and bills were paid - that I missed many precious moments to connect with my kids when they were young.

It wasn't until later in life that I truly understood something profound: the bond between a father and child isn't just about fulfilling a duty - it's a precious gift that shapes how your children see themselves and their entire world. When you build close connections with your kids, you're helping them develop their self-image, understand their place in the world, and learn how to form healthy relationships throughout their lives.

If I could go back and do it all over, I would have approached fatherhood differently from day one. I would have set intentional goals driven by courage, fortitude, faith, and love to become the best dad I could be. These aren't just nice ideas - they're the building blocks of lasting connections that strengthen the father-child bond. This isn't another task on your to-do list; it's both an incredible privilege and a powerful investment in your family's future. Don't wait like I did - start building these bonds today.

WHAT THE BIBLE SAYS ABOUT
THE FATHER-CHILD RELATIONSHIP

The Bible reveals four essential roles that earthly fathers are called to fulfill, mirroring our Heavenly Father's perfect example discussed in chapter two.

Fathers as Protectors

Just as God is our shield and fortress (Psalm 18:2), fathers are called to protect their children both physically and spiritually. Like Job, who regularly offered sacrifices on behalf of his children (Job 1:5), fathers must guard their children's spiritual wellbeing. This protective role extends to teaching discernment and wisdom, as Solomon counseled in Proverbs 4:1-6.

Fathers as Order Keepers

God is not a God of disorder but of peace (1 Corinthians 14:33). Similarly, fathers establish godly order in their homes. Moses demonstrated this when he appointed judges and established clear guidelines for the Israelites (Exodus 18:17-23). This role includes setting boundaries, maintaining discipline, and creating structure that allows children to flourish.

Fathers as Providers

Our Heavenly Father provides for all our needs (Philippians 4:19). Earthly fathers reflect this by providing not just physical necessities but also spiritual nourishment. As Jesus taught in Matthew 7:9-11, good fathers give good gifts to their children. This provision includes wisdom, guidance, and spiritual instruction, as emphasized in Deuteronomy 6:6-7.

Fathers as Stabilizers

God is our rock and firm foundation (Psalm 18:2). Like Abraham, who demonstrated unwavering faith that stabilized his family's spiritual journey (Romans 4:20-21), fathers provide emotional and spiritual stability. This role involves being consistently present, emotionally available, and spiritually steadfast, creating a secure environment where children can grow in faith and confidence.

UNDERSTANDING HOW NEEDS VARY BY GENDER AND AGE

I remember sitting in my study late one night, overwhelmed by the different needs of my four children. My teenage son was wrestling with peer pressure at school, while my youngest daughter just wanted to have tea parties with her daddy. I kept asking myself: How could one father be everything to each child?

Through countless prayers and years of experience (including plenty of mistakes), I discovered something crucial: understanding our children's unique needs isn't just helpful—it's absolutely essential to being the father God has called us to be.

You see, while every child is uniquely created in God's image, there are certain patterns that can help us better connect with our kids at different stages of their lives. Just as our Heavenly Father meets each of us exactly where we are, we need to adapt our approach to meet our children's changing needs. Let me share what I've learned from raising my two sons and two daughters—it might help you avoid some of the late-night worry sessions I had.

FATHERING SONS

Let me tell you about a breakthrough moment I had with my son. He was 13 and having trouble in school. My first instinct was to lecture him, but then I remembered something important from my own childhood - how my dad taught me life lessons while we worked on cars together. So one Saturday, I invited my son to help me change the oil in the family van. As we worked side by side, something magical happened. Without any pressure, he started opening up about feeling like he had to act tough at school to fit in and did not feel like he had any friends. That simple afternoon of car maintenance turned into a beautiful opportunity to talk about what real strength looks like - the kind Jesus showed us.

You see, our sons are looking to us to understand what it means to be godly men. They desperately need our approval and encouragement - it's like water for their souls, helping them grow in confidence and self-worth. And while they need to see us as strong role models, they also need to see us express our emotions honestly. I've learned that when I share my own feelings appropriately, it gives my sons permission to do the same.

One of the most important things we can do as fathers is set clear, loving boundaries. This becomes especially crucial during those turbulent teenage years when hormones are raging and every boundary gets tested. I've seen firsthand how boys without strong father figures often struggle more with behavior issues and negative peer pressure. Through our daily actions and gentle guidance, we teach our sons how to respect women, handle their emotions, and grow into men of God.

FATHERING DAUGHTERS

I'll never forget the evening my teenage daughter knocked on my office door, her voice shaky as she asked if we could talk. We settled onto the old porch swing - the same one where we'd shared ice cream cones and silly stories when she was little. This time, she confided her fears about an upcoming class presentation. Instead of jumping in with solutions, I remembered how sometimes the best thing a father can do is just be present.

"Remember when you were small," I said, gently pushing the swing, "and you'd climb up to the top of that big slide at the park? You were scared then too, but you knew I was standing at the bottom to catch you." Her eyes lit up with recognition. "You'd always catch me, no matter what," she said softly. "That's right," I replied, "and while I can't give this speech for you, I'm still your safety net. Always will be."

Through raising both my sons and daughters, I've learned that each relationship needs its own special touch. My wife has been my greatest teacher in understanding our daughters' hearts. She helped me see that every interaction with our girls either builds them up or tears them down - there's no neutral ground. As their first model of how a man should treat them, my words and actions were shaping their expectations for every future relationship.

This hit home hard when my younger daughter didn't make the tennis team. My first instinct was pure dad-mode: problem solve, suggest private coaching, map out a training schedule. But what she really needed was for me to sit beside her, listen to her hurt, and remind her that her worth had nothing to do with making any team. It came from being deeply loved - both by her earthly father and her Heavenly one.

Through these experiences, I've discovered that daughters need their fathers to be:

> - Trustworthy confidants who listen without judgment
> - Protectors who help them feel secure while encouraging independence
> - Living examples of how godly men treat women with respect
> - Steady sources of unconditional love and support

I've learned something powerful over the years - our kids are always watching how we treat their mom. When my daughter saw me bringing tea to her mother in bed, or heard me speaking to her with patience during disagreements, she was learning what to expect from men in her own life. Every time we show respect, kindness, and genuine care for our wives, we're teaching our children what healthy relationships look like. It's not just about words - it's about living out love in ways they can see and understand every single day.

THE VITAL ROLE OF THE FATHER

A father's presence shapes his children's lives in powerful ways. When you show up consistently and love your kids unconditionally, you help them feel secure and protected. Your encouragement and support build their confidence and sense of self-worth, whether you're raising sons or daughters.

Think about Moses's father, who trusted God enough to place his son in that basket on the Nile. Consider Joseph, who adopted Jesus as his own and taught Him the carpenter's trade. These biblical fathers remind us that our role isn't just about providing food and shelter - it's about creating a foundation of faith, security, and love that will support our children throughout their lives.

When you show up consistently and love your kids unconditionally, you reflect God's unwavering commitment to His children. Every soccer match you attend, every bedtime story you read, every tough conversation you navigate - these moments aren't just items on your calendar. They're building blocks of your children's emotional and spiritual foundation.

I learned this lesson profoundly when my son was struggling with his faith during his sophomore year of college. Those years of consistent presence - the breakfast discussions, the time playing basketball together, the times he spent with me at my job - had laid a foundation strong enough to weather his doubts. He knew he could bring his questions to me because I had always been there, just as our Heavenly Father is always there for us.

Your role as a father includes:

> Being your children's first and most important teacher of God's truth
> Showing them through your actions what it means to live with integrity

- Demonstrating how to handle both success and failure with grace
- Creating a safe harbor where they can always return for guidance and support

If you don't step into this vital role of teaching and guiding, the world will gladly fill the void - and often with messages that contradict our biblical values. Your active involvement directly impacts your child's future success, not just in worldly terms, but in their spiritual journey as well.

Remember, the relationship between a father and child isn't just about today's challenges or tomorrow's achievements. It's about building a legacy of faith, love, and wisdom that will influence generations to come. When you invest time and energy in these precious bonds, you're not just strengthening your family - you're participating in God's design for fatherhood. This is what truly matters in developing a strong bond with your child and forms the cornerstone of Fathering Strong.

TEACHING CORE VALUES - BUILDING CHARACTER AND LEAVING A LEGACY

One crisp autumn morning, I took my children hiking on a challenging mountain trail. As we faced steep climbs and uncertain footing, I realized this journey perfectly mirrored our path of teaching values - sometimes difficult, requiring persistence, but ultimately rewarding. When my youngest wanted to turn back, her older brother encouraged her with words I'd often used with him: "Remember what Dad always says - we can do hard things when we trust God to give us strength."

Teaching values isn't a one-time conversation or a yearly lecture - it's a daily commitment to living out our faith and principles in ways our children can see, understand, and eventually embrace as their own. Just as God instructed the Israelites to teach their children "when you sit at home and when you walk along the road, when you lie down and when you get up" (Deuteronomy 6:7), we must weave character building into the fabric of everyday life.

The core virtues of courage, fortitude, faith, and love aren't just concepts to memorize - they're living principles that shape who our children become. Here's how to teach these values effectively at different ages.

Young Children (Ages 2-5)

At this tender age, children are like sponges, absorbing everything they see and hear. I remember teaching my toddler daughter about courage through her fear of thunderstorms. Instead of dismissing her fears, we turned them into opportunities to trust God, praying together and reading about Jesus calming the storm. Simple activities that build character include:

> - Reading Bible stories about brave characters
> - Practicing persistence with age-appropriate challenges
> - Making bedtime prayers a consistent routine
> - Celebrating small acts of kindness and bravery

Elementary School (Ages 6-11)

During these formative years, children begin to understand deeper concepts of right and wrong. When my son stood up for a classmate being bullied, it opened a beautiful discussion about moral courage and loving our neighbors. Key teaching opportunities include:

> - Discussing moral choices in daily situations
> - Setting achievable goals that require effort
> - Participating in family service projects
> - Having meaningful conversations about faith and values

Middle School (Ages 12-14)

These years can test both faith and family bonds. I remember when my son started questioning everything he'd been taught. Instead of shutting down his doubts, we used them as springboards for deeper discussions about faith. One evening, his challenging questions about prayer led to one of our most meaningful conversations about God's faithfulness in our lives. During these transformative years, focus on:

> Building courage to resist peer pressure through biblical examples like Daniel
> Strengthening fortitude through academic and personal challenges
> Encouraging personal Bible study and authentic prayer life
> Demonstrating love through patience and understanding during emotional ups and downs

High School (Ages 15-18)

As our children prepare to leave the nest, our role shifts from direct instruction to trusted guidance. When my daughter struggled with choosing a college, we returned to the values we'd taught her: seeking God's wisdom through prayer, showing courage in facing uncertainty, and maintaining faith even when the path isn't clear. Help teens develop:

> Courage to make independent decisions aligned with biblical principles
> Fortitude as they face college preparations and life choices
> A deeper, personal faith through theological discussions and spiritual exploration
> Understanding of God's unconditional love as they navigate increasing independence

Teaching Values to Sons - Building warriors for Christ

Boys need to understand that true strength flows from godly character. I learned this lesson when my son's basketball team lost a crucial game. Instead of focusing on the defeat, we discussed how Joseph maintained his integrity even in prison. Help your sons develop:

> Emotional strength rooted in biblical masculinity
> Respect for women modeled after Christ's treatment of women

- ▸ Accountability for choices while experiencing God's grace
- ▸ Understanding that real men seek God's wisdom and help

Teaching Values to Daughters - Nurturing Women of Faith

Girls flourish when they understand their worth comes from being daughters of the King. When my daughter felt pressured to compromise her values to fit in, we explored Queen Esther's courage to stand firm in her beliefs. Guide your daughters in:

- ▸ Building confidence based on their identity in Christ
- ▸ Understanding their value extends far beyond physical appearance
- ▸ Developing discernment in relationships through biblical wisdom
- ▸ Finding their voice while maintaining godly character

Let me share a story that really brings these principles to life. Both my kids faced the classic teenage challenge growing up - pressure to attend parties where there'd be drinking. What happened next showed me that all those years of talking about values had really sunk in, though in beautifully different ways.

My son handled it head-on, in his typical straightforward style. When invited, he simply said, "Thanks, but that's not my scene," and explained why his faith guided him away from underage drinking. No drama, no judgment - just quiet confidence in his convictions.

My daughter took a different approach, just as effective but uniquely her own. She suggested hosting a movie night at our house instead. She found a way to maintain her friendships while staying true to her values. I remember feeling so proud watching her navigate that situation with such wisdom and grace.

You know what really struck me? Both responses reflected our family's values, but in ways that matched their individual personalities. It wasn't about following a script - it was about them owning their faith and making it real in their own ways.

Here's what I've learned through it all: teaching values isn't about raising perfect kids. It's about pointing them to a perfect God. Every stumble becomes a chance to show grace, every challenge an opportunity to build character, and every victory a moment to celebrate God's faithfulness in our lives.

EFFECTIVE COMMUNICATION AND ACTIVE LISTENING: CONNECTING WITH YOUR CHILDREN

Let me share something that changed everything about how I talk with my kids. One night, my teenage son and I had gotten into it pretty badly. You know the kind - voices raised, doors slammed. I was standing outside his room, my hand raised to knock, when that still, small voice reminded me of James 1:19: "Be quick to listen, slow to speak, slow to anger."

It hit me like a ton of bricks. Here I was, ready to barge in with another lecture, when what my son really needed was for me to listen. Really listen - the way our Heavenly Father listens to us when we pray. Not just waiting for my turn to talk, but truly trying to understand what was in his heart.

That moment transformed how I communicate with all my children. I started thinking about how Jesus listened to people - how He gave them His full attention, asked thoughtful questions, and really heard what they were saying beneath their words. I wanted to be that kind of father.

Let me share what I've learned about connecting with kids at different ages - because believe me, what works with a toddler won't cut it with a teenager!

Ages 2-5

Keep things simple and clear. Use short sentences and lots of praise.

> ‣ Examples: Read stories together, play make-believe, and use simple words with pictures. Be patient, repeat things as needed, and maintain a warm, friendly voice.

> ‣ Listening Tips: Get down to their eye level and make eye contact when they speak. Use encouraging phrases like "I see" or "Uh-huh." Help them label emotions by saying things like "You seem sad" or "That made you happy!"

Ages 6-11

Children this age are ready for deeper conversations. Encourage them to express their thoughts and feelings.

> ‣ Examples: Start conversations with open-ended questions like "What was the best part of your day?" Explain the reasoning behind rules and welcome their opinions, even if you disagree.
> ‣ Listening Tips: Make eye contact, nod to show engagement, and reflect their words back to them. Ask follow-up questions to better understand their perspective.

Ages 12-14

Teens face significant changes. Show patience and understanding.

> ‣ Examples: Create safe spaces for difficult conversations. Respect their need for privacy. Listen without judgment and guide rather than control.
> ‣ Listening Tips: Give undivided attention by putting away distractions like phones. Validate their feelings and ask questions that encourage them to elaborate.

Ages 15-18

Support their transition to adulthood by encouraging independence.

> ‣ Examples: Treat them as equals in conversations. Offer advice only when requested. Support their independence and goals while maintaining open communication.

> Listening Tips: Show respect when listening and share your perspective when asked. Avoid unsolicited advice and demonstrate trust in their decision-making abilities.

Communicating with Sons - Building Trust Through Action

I learned something fascinating about communicating with my son - he opened up most when we were doing something together, side by side, rather than sitting face-to-face. One Saturday afternoon, while we were washing the van, he suddenly started telling me about the pressure he was feeling at school to try drugs. That conversation might never have happened if I'd tried to force it across the kitchen table. There's something about working together that helps boys feel safe enough to share what's really on their hearts.

Here are some practical applications to better communications with your son:

> Engage in activities together while talking
> Use sports or shared interests as conversation bridges
> Respect their need for shorter, more direct communications
> Share your own experiences with manhood and faith
> Create opportunities for "man-to-man" talks

Communicating with Daughters: Nurturing Heart Connections

I'll never forget the breakthrough I had with my teenage daughter. We started having regular "coffee dates" at this little café downtown - just the two of us. Something magical happened when she knew she had my complete attention, when my phone was tucked away and I was fully present. Over steaming cups of hot chocolate (her) and coffee (me), she began sharing what was going on in her life. Those moments taught me that daughters need to feel emotionally safe and valued before they'll truly open up.

Here are some effective strategies for communicating with your daughter:

- Create regular one-on-one time for heart-to-heart talks
- Listen attentively to small details - they often lead to bigger discussions
- Show genuine interest in their thoughts and feelings
- Validate their emotions while gently guiding their responses
- Maintain consistent availability, especially during difficult times

I learned the power of these approaches during a particularly challenging season with my children. My son was struggling with peer pressure about dating, while my daughter was dealing with social media drama. Though their issues were different, both situations required me to:

- Listen without judgment
- Share relevant biblical principles gently
- Ask guiding questions rather than lecture
- Pray with them about their challenges
- Follow up consistently to show ongoing support

Remember, effective communication isn't about having all the answers - it's about creating an environment where your children feel safe sharing their hearts. Just as our Heavenly Father welcomes all our prayers, we must welcome all our children's thoughts and feelings, even when they're challenging to hear.

QUALITY TIME: MAKING MEMORIES THAT LAST FOREVER

The day my son caught his first fish, his excitement wasn't really about the fish – it was about the hours we'd spent together learning, trying, and finally succeeding. Just as God walks alongside us in our daily journey, we're called to be present in our children's lives, not just physically, but emotionally and spiritually.

Consider how Jesus invested time in His disciples – He didn't just teach them; He lived life alongside them, sharing meals, walking together, and experiencing both joys and challenges. This models how we should approach quality time with our children: being fully present, engaged, and intentional.

Quality time means more than occupying the same space – it requires giving our children our undivided attention. When I finally learned to put my phone away during family dinner, our conversations improved. Sometimes the most profound connections happen in ordinary moments when we're truly present, just as God is present in every moment of our lives.

Let me share specific ways to spend quality time with your children at different ages, remembering that each stage of development requires its own unique approach to building meaningful connections:

Ages 2-5 - Building Wonder and Trust

These early years lay the foundation for how your children will view both their earthly and heavenly Father. Some of my most precious memories include:

> - Reading stories with different voices for each character
> - Going on "adventure walks" to discover God's creation
> - Having special daddy-child sneak-out dates where I would take one of the kids after bedtime when everyone else was asleep, and we would "sneak out" for donuts.
> - Playing imagination games and hide-and-seek

Ages 6-11 - Nurturing Curiosity and Connection

During these formative years, children begin to develop deeper interests and questions about life and faith. Meaningful activities include:

> - Teaching life skills while sharing wisdom
> - Starting a family game night tradition
> - Working on service projects together

- ▸ Attending their sports events or performances
- ▸ Having "learning adventures" that combine fun with board games or playing video games together

Ages 12-14 - Building Bridges During Change

These transitional years can feel like navigating stormy waters, but they also offer unique opportunities for deeper connection. I remember when my daughter started pulling away, feeling too "grown up" for our traditional daddy-daughter dates. Instead of forcing our old routine, we found new ways to connect through shared interests in photography and hiking. These years call for:

- ▸ Creating new traditions that respect their growing maturity
- ▸ Finding shared hobbies or interests to explore together
- ▸ Making time for meaningful conversations during everyday activities
- ▸ Attending their events and showing genuine interest in their passions
- ▸ Planning special one-on-one outings that feel more "grown-up"

Ages 15-18 - Preparing for Launch

As children prepare for independence, quality time takes on new significance. When my son was preparing for college, our weekend car maintenance sessions became precious opportunities to discuss life, faith, and his future. Focus on:

- ▸ Treating them more like adults while maintaining parental guidance
- ▸ Teaching practical life skills alongside spiritual wisdom
- ▸ Creating regular check-in times that feel natural and respectful
- ▸ Supporting their interests while sharing your expertise
- ▸ Making space for deeper discussions about faith, purpose, and future plans

Quality Time with Sons: Building Bonds Through Action

Boys often connect best through shared activities. I discovered this truth when my son seemed distant and unreachable until we started playing tennis together. Those matches became a time to talk about everything from school pressures to dating, and our periodic hikes at local nature reserves gave us even more opportunities to discuss life's deeper questions while enjoying God's creation. Consider:

> Engaging in physical activities or sports together
> Teaching practical skills while sharing life lessons
> Working on projects that require cooperation
> Having regular "man-to-man" time for deeper discussions
> Creating adventures that build confidence and trust

Quality Time with Daughters: Nurturing Heart Connections

Daughters often thrive on emotional connection and focused attention. My youngest daughter and I discovered our best talks happened during our bike rides on local bike trails. Try:

> Planning special daddy-daughter dates
> Creating traditions that make them feel cherished
> Finding ways to serve others together
> Making time for both fun activities and heart-to-heart talks
> Showing interest in their world while sharing yours

REAL-LIFE EXAMPLES THAT WORKED

Joshua, a dad in one of the Fathering Strong groups and a firefighter, started a tradition of "Breakfast with Dad" Saturday mornings on the weekends when he was off duty. What began as simple pancake-making with his young children evolved into deep conversations about faith and life as they grew older. Even now, his adult children make time for these breakfast connections when they're home.

Another father, Mike, learned to connect with his teenage son through their shared interest in running. Their weekend jogs became a time where his son would open up about school pressures and faith questions. "Something about running together," Mike shared, "made it easier for him to talk about hard things."

David, a single father, made it his mission to attend every one of his daughter's dance recitals, not just watching but helping her practice at home. These practice sessions created opportunities for him to teach her about perseverance, excellence, and using her gifts for God's glory.

Remember that some of the most impactful moments aren't planned – they happen in the ordinary spaces of life when we're simply available and attentive. Just as God uses everyday moments to teach and shape us, we can use daily activities to build lasting connections with our children.

The key is being intentional about creating opportunities while remaining flexible enough to embrace unexpected moments of connection. Whether it's a planned camping trip or an impromptu late-night conversation, these times of focused attention show our children they're valued and loved.

DISCIPLINE: TEACHING YOUR CHILDREN RIGHT FROM WRONG

One evening, after harshly scolding my son over a failed math test, I sat in my study feeling ashamed. My reaction had been more about my frustration than his learning. As I watched him shuffle dejectedly to his room, I realized I had just damaged our relationship instead of teaching him responsibility. As I prayed for wisdom afterward, Ephesians 6:4 echoed in my mind: "Fathers, do not exasperate your children; instead, bring them up in the training and instruction of the Lord." I realized that godly discipline isn't about controlling behavior – it's about shaping hearts.

Biblical Foundation for Loving Discipline

Just as our Heavenly Father disciplines those He loves (Hebrews 12:6), we're called to guide our children with both firmness and grace. Consider these biblical principles:

> Discipline flows from love (Proverbs 13:24)
> The goal is wisdom and character (Proverbs 22:6)
> Correction should restore, not destroy (Galatians 6:1)
> Grace and truth work together (John 1:17)

The heart of Fathering Strong discipline teaches our children not just what is right, but why it's right. When my daughter lied about completing her homework, rather than just punishing her, we explored why honesty matters to God and how deception damages trust. This approach helps children develop:

> Internal motivation rather than external compliance
> Understanding of God's character and values
> Wisdom to make good choices independently
> A healthy response to authority

Let me share how these principles work at different ages:

Ages 2-5 - Foundation Years

During these early years, consistency and clarity are crucial. I learned this when my youngest would throw tantrums in public. By calmly maintaining boundaries while showing love, we taught her that our standards (and God's love) remained constant regardless of her behavior. Focus on:

> Clear, simple rules with immediate, age-appropriate consequences
> Brief explanations they can understand
> Lots of praise for good choices
> Physical comfort after discipline to reinforce love
> Regular reminders of God's love and forgiveness

Ages 6-11 - Building Understanding

These years offer rich opportunities to connect behavior with biblical principles. When my son was caught copying a friend's homework, we used this mistake to explore integrity and its importance in God's eyes. During these formative years:

> ‣ Move from simple rules to understanding principles
> ‣ Help them see the natural consequences of choices
> ‣ Use Scripture to guide discussions about behavior
> ‣ Implement consistent consequences while showing grace
> ‣ Encourage self-reflection and personal responsibility

Ages 12-14 - Navigating Changes

The middle school years often test both faith and family rules. I remember when my daughter started pushing boundaries with social media usage. Instead of simply imposing restrictions, we had meaningful conversations about the serious risks - like stalking and bullying - and discussed how social media can negatively impact mental health. Together, we explored healthy ways to steward our time and protect our hearts while staying connected. During these challenging years:

> ‣ Connect rules to real-world consequences
> ‣ Guide them through decision-making processes
> ‣ Allow appropriate natural consequences
> ‣ Maintain boundaries while respecting growing independence
> ‣ Use mistakes as opportunities for spiritual growth

Ages 15-18 - Preparing for Independence

These years require a delicate balance between maintaining authority and fostering independence. When my son broke curfew, instead of just grounding him, we discussed trust, responsibility, and how his choices affected others. Focus on:

> Treating them more as young adults while maintaining clear boundaries
> Explaining the "why" behind family standards
> Allowing them to experience natural consequences
> Teaching decision-making skills through real situations
> Connecting choices to future outcomes

Disciplining Sons: Building Honorable Men

Boys often need clear boundaries with logical consequences. I learned this when dealing with my son's aggressive behavior on the basketball court. Through this challenge, we explored biblical manhood and controlling our strength. Remember to:

> Set clear expectations with defined consequences
> Address issues directly and calmly
> Connect discipline to character development
> Use physical activity constructively
> Model emotional self-control

Disciplining Daughters: Nurturing Godly Women

Girls often need emotional security within boundaries. When my daughter struggled with mean girl dynamics, we focused on identity in Christ and treating others with kindness. Essential approaches include:

> Balance emotional support with clear standards
> Address heart issues behind behavior
> Help them process feelings while maintaining boundaries

- ➤ Guide social interactions with wisdom
- ➤ Model respectful communication

REAL-LIFE LEARNING MOMENTS

Let me share two pivotal moments that shaped my approach to discipline

The first came when my son was caught lying about his phone usage. My initial anger could have damaged our relationship, but instead, we:

- ➤ Took time to cool down (James 1:19)
- ➤ Discussed why honesty matters to God
- ➤ Explored the root causes of his deception
- ➤ Established new boundaries together
- ➤ Prayed for wisdom and strength

The second occurred with my daughter's disrespectful attitude. Rather than just punishing the behavior, we:

- ➤ Created a safe space to share feelings
- ➤ Examined Scripture about honoring parents
- ➤ Developed better communication strategies
- ➤ Set clear expectations for respect
- ➤ Showed grace while maintaining standards

Let me tell you something I've learned the hard way about discipline - it's like walking a tightrope. You've got to stay steady and balanced, adjusting your approach for each child and situation while keeping your eyes fixed on what really matters: helping your kids grow more like Jesus.

I've found that the key is being consistent with consequences while staying flexible in how we handle each situation. And you know what? It's not really about getting them to behave perfectly - it's about pointing them to their perfect Savior. When we discipline our kids with genuine love and God-given wisdom, we're showing them a glimpse of how our Heavenly Father loves and guides us. That's what transforms hearts.

CREATING SMART GOALS FOR STRENGTHENING THE BOND WITH YOUR CHILDREN

Just like we need clear plans at work, building stronger relationships with our kids needs real intention behind it. I've found that using SMART goals helps turn those "I should spend more time with the kids" thoughts into actual moments that matter. And when we combine practical planning with our core virtues - that's when the magic happens.

Think about it - it takes courage to step out of our comfort zones and be vulnerable with our children. We need fortitude to keep showing up consistently, even when we're tired or discouraged. Our faith guides every decision and reminds us of this sacred calling we have as dads. And love? Well, that's the heartbeat of it all, making sure everything we do builds up rather than tears down.

Let me share some specific goals I've seen work wonders in helping dads create deeper connections with their kids. These aren't just nice ideas - they're practical steps that can transform your relationship with your children.

Teaching Values

- Lead a 30-minute family devotion every Sunday at 7pm, covering one specific virtue per month with real-life examples and action steps
- Create a "Growth Journal" where each family member records one honest mistake weekly and what they learned, reviewing together each Friday evening
- Complete one family service project each quarter, spending at least 4 hours helping a specific local charity

Effective Communication Instead of: "Talk more with my kids"
SMART Goals:

➤ Schedule individual "heart check" conversations every Sunday evening
➤ Practice active listening by asking at least two follow-up questions before offering advice
➤ Create phone-free zones during dinner and car rides
➤ Keep a prayer journal for each child's specific concerns

Quality Time Goals Instead of: "Spend more time with the kids"
SMART Goals:

➤ Schedule monthly one-on-one "adventure days" with each child
➤ Attend 100% of their major events (games, recitals, performances)
➤ Create weekly family game nights every Friday from 7-9 PM
➤ Plan quarterly family service projects at local charities

Discipline and Guidance Instead of: "Be a better disciplinarian"
SMART Goals:

➤ Review family rules and consequences quarterly
➤ Implement 10-minute cooling-off periods before addressing major infractions
➤ Hold weekly family meetings to discuss challenges and victories
➤ Create behavior charts that emphasize character growth over mere compliance

Age-Specific Goal Setting

For Young Children (Ages 2-5)

➤ Read one Bible story every night before bed
➤ Spend 15 minutes of focused playtime daily
➤ Practice one new prayer together weekly
➤ Create monthly photo memories of special moments

For Elementary Ages (6-11)

- ➤ Teach one life skill monthly
- ➤ Have weekly "walk and talk" times
- ➤ Start a shared devotional journal
- ➤ Create opportunities for serving others together

For Middle School (12-14)

- ➤ Schedule monthly mentor meetings
- ➤ Create technology-free connection times
- ➤ Develop shared interests or hobbies
- ➤ Plan regular service projects together

For High School (15-18)

- ➤ Hold monthly guidance sessions for future planning
- ➤ Create leadership opportunities within family
- ➤ Schedule regular college/career exploration talks
- ➤ Plan meaningful rites of passage experiences

Remember, the ultimate goal isn't perfect execution of our plans – it's drawing our children closer to God while strengthening family bonds. As Proverbs 16:9 reminds us, "In their hearts humans plan their course, but the Lord establishes their steps."

HOW STRONG FATHER-CHILD BONDS HELP KIDS GROW

Let me share something powerful I've witnessed over decades of fathering: when we pour ourselves into building strong bonds with our children - really living out those core strengths of courage, fortitude, faith, and love - we're doing so much more than creating happy memories. We're actually showing our kids a living picture of how God loves His children.

You know what amazes me? Modern research keeps confirming what Scripture has taught all along. Just as our Heavenly Father's presence transforms our lives (James 4:8), an engaged earthly father shapes his children in profound ways.

Think about spiritual growth. I've seen it in my own family and countless others - when fathers actively disciple their children, just as Paul mentored Timothy (2 Timothy 1:5), kids are far more likely to embrace faith as their own. They grasp God's unconditional love more deeply because they've experienced it through their dad. They approach God confidently as "Abba, Father" because they understand what a loving father looks like.

But it goes beyond spiritual impact. Remember how Jesus provided that sense of security that enabled His disciples to step out in faith? Similarly, when we build strong bonds with our kids, we're giving them an emotional foundation that boosts their confidence, helps them handle stress better, and equips them to build healthy relationships of their own. It's beautiful to see how this security often leads to better grades, stronger problem-solving skills, and more resilience in facing life's challenges.

Just as God designed family relationships to reflect His character (Ephesians 3:14-15), these father-child bonds shape how our kids relate to others. Sons learn to father by watching us model Christ-like leadership and tenderness. Daughters develop a deep understanding of their worth in God's eyes and learn to expect the respect they deserve in relationships.

Here's what I want you to remember: your role as a father isn't just important - **it's irreplaceable.** Just as our Heavenly Father's love uniquely shapes us, your presence in your children's lives creates ripples that will impact generations. This isn't about being perfect - it's about being present, being faithful, and pointing our children to the perfect Father who guides us all.

PART 3

LIVING THE FATHERING STRONG LIFE

I've explored the four core virtues and six foundational strengths of Fathering Strong where SMART goals build their foundation, I feel like we're ready for something more. We've done the planning, we've laid the groundwork, but now – now it's time for the real heart of what we're doing here: actually living the Fathering Strong life.

Just as Solomon reminds us in Proverbs 16:9, "In their hearts humans plan their course, but the Lord establishes their steps." This journey isn't about reaching some final destination – it's about walking faithfully each day, one step at a time.

I'll be honest with you – I used to be that dad who was so laser-focused on checking boxes and hitting milestones that I nearly missed the miracle happening right in front of me. I was drowning in "shoulds" – you know the ones I'm talking about. I should spend more time, should be more patient, should be more successful... Sound familiar?

But then God opened my eyes to something beautiful. I learned to embrace the joy in the moment. Those giggles during bedtime stories became my worship. The warmth of my son's hand in mine became my prayer. Watching my daughter overcome challenges became my testimony of God's faithfulness.

In this final part of our journey together, I want to show you how to weave these core strengths into the fabric of your daily life, just as we're called to weave God's commands into our lives. We'll talk about building resilience – not just the world's version, but the kind Paul speaks of when he says, "I can do all things through Christ who strengthens me" (Philippians 4:13). We'll explore the power of community because as Ecclesiastes 4:9-10 tells us, "Two are better than one... if either of them falls down, one can help the other up."

But perhaps most importantly, we'll focus on leaving a legacy that echoes through generations, just as Abraham's faithfulness blessed not just Isaac, but countless generations to come. How can we live with such courage, fortitude, faith, and love that we don't just impact our children, but create ripples that touch future generations?

This isn't about striving for perfection or following some rigid rulebook. It's about developing a heart that beats in rhythm with God's purpose for fathers. It's about embracing the adventure and celebrating the journey of fatherhood.

Are you ready? Let's step into these final chapters together and discover what it truly means to be Fathering Strong.

CHAPTER 14

PUTTING IT ALL TOGETHER - LINKING GOALS TO FATHERING STRONG

Let me share something I've learned over the years: becoming a stronger father is a lot like coaching a winning team. Just as a championship football team relies on the perfect combination of offense, defense, and special teams working together, becoming a stronger father requires mastering and integrating multiple elements. The six core areas we've explored – physical health, spiritual growth, emotional well-being, financial stability, marriage relationships, and connecting with children – are like key players on your team, each with a crucial role to play. These areas are strengthened and unified by the four core virtues of Fathering Strong: courage to face challenges, fortitude to persevere, faith to guide our path, and love to bind everything together.

I've seen it time and time again – when these pieces click together, something magical happens. The discipline you build at the gym somehow makes you mentally tougher. Your prayer time deepens your faith and gives you courage. As you grow emotionally, you find yourself loving more deeply. When you get your finances in order, you have the freedom to really show up for your family. And both your marriage and your relationship with your kids? They flourish because you're bringing your whole, healthy self to the table.

Here's the thing – you don't have to master everything at once. It's about understanding how all these pieces fit together to create something beautiful: strong, purposeful fatherhood.

I remember hitting rock bottom when my kids were young. Working insane hours left me exhausted, my health suffered, and I'd lose my temper over the tiniest things with my children. Then everything changed when I finally started prioritizing self-care – making better food choices and getting regular exercise. The transformation was life changing: my energy came flooding back, and with it, my patience. Playing with my kids transformed from a draining obligation into pure joy – the best part of each day. I'll forever be grateful to my wife for standing by me through it all, offering gentle guidance, and being our family's foundation when I couldn't be.

In this chapter, we'll explore how these strengths work together, just like a championship team in action. Think of yourself as the head coach, coordinating your offensive line of physical and spiritual growth with your defensive line of emotional and financial stability. Your special teams? That's your marriage and connection with your kids – ready to make those game-changing plays? As you develop one aspect of your game plan and begin your journey to becoming Fathering Strong, you'll see how it naturally elevates the performance of your life, your family's life, and the community in which you live.

I'll give you practical, doable ways to weave these strengths into your everyday life, from simple morning prayers to fun family game nights. We'll talk about staying flexible too, because let's face it – life rarely goes according to plan.

Most importantly, this chapter is about embracing the journey. It's about celebrating those small wins, learning from the times we stumble, and finding joy in the simple moments with our kids. It's about nurturing that incredible bond you have with your children and watching it grow stronger every day.

This is where everything we've talked about comes together. When you understand how these strengths support each other and live with courage, fortitude, faith, and love, you won't just become a better father – you'll discover a life filled with meaning and lasting joy.

MAKING THESE STRENGTHS PART OF EVERY DAY

To make the six foundational strengths part of your life, you need to plan ahead and set clear goals you can reach. You don't have to be perfect - just try to get better in each area. Here are some tips:

Prioritize and schedule

Treat each foundational strength like an important appointment on your calendar. Schedule time for exercise, prayer or meditation, quality time with your spouse and kids, financial planning, and personal reflection.

> ➤ Find activities that address multiple strengths at once: Going for a hike with your family strengthens physical health and family bonds while providing time for spiritual reflection. Similarly, joining a faith-based fitness group combines physical, spiritual, and social elements.
> ➤ Start small and be consistent: Don't try to change everything overnight. Start with small, manageable steps and focus on doing them consistently. Over time, these small changes will add up to significant progress.
> ➤ Be flexible and adaptable: Life doesn't always go according to plan. Be willing to adjust your schedule and priorities as needed. The key is to maintain a balanced approach over the long term, not to achieve perfection in any given day.
> ➤ Seek support and accountability: Share your goals with your spouse, a friend, or a mentor. Having someone to support and hold you accountable can make a big difference.
> ➤ Practice self-compassion: Be kind to yourself and acknowledge that you will have setbacks. Don't let occasional lapses derail your progress. Simply pick yourself up and keep moving forward.

CREATING A BALANCED APPROACH TO FATHERHOOD

A balanced approach to fatherhood means prioritizing all aspects of your life - your physical, spiritual, emotional, and financial well-being, along with your relationships with your spouse and children. These areas are deeply interconnected, and when one suffers, the others often follow.

Being a strong father means staying present, engaged, and intentional in every role you play - husband, father, and individual. It requires leading with courage, fortitude, faith, and love, qualities we explored deeply in part 1 of the book.

While every week brings different challenges and opportunities, here's a practical framework for integrating the foundational strengths into your routine:

Daily: Brief prayer/meditation, nutritious meals, one-on-one time with each child (even just 5-10 minutes makes a difference).

3 times per week: Exercise (30-45 minutes), meaningful connection with your spouse (real conversation, shared activities).

Weekly: Extended spiritual practice (church, small group, or personal study), family bonding activity (game night, outdoor adventure), financial check-in (budget review, bills).

Monthly: Dedicated date night with your spouse, family meeting to align goals and communicate openly, review of long-term plans and progress.

TAKE YOUR TIME IN MAKING CHANGE

Look, I get it - looking at this whole framework might feel overwhelming. Trust me, I've been there. When I first started my journey to become a better father, I tried to change everything at once. You know what happened? I crashed and burned. And I'm not alone - I've seen countless dads make the same mistake.

Here's what I've learned: start small and be patient. Pick just one or two things that matter most to you right now. Maybe it's reading a bedtime story to your kids every night, or finally starting that morning workout routine. Whatever you choose, give it time to stick - about three weeks or so. That's when it starts feeling natural, like brushing your teeth.

Once those first changes become part of who you are, then you can add something new. It's like building a house - you need a solid foundation before adding the next floor. Take it from someone who's been there - this steady approach might feel slow at first, but it leads to real, lasting change that transforms not just you, but your whole family's life.

Remember, being a stronger father isn't about becoming perfect overnight. It's about making small, intentional changes that add up to something beautiful - a life rich with purpose, balance, and deep connections with the people you love most.

SETTING SMART GOALS DOES WORK

We've talked about SMART goals throughout this book - those specific, measurable, achievable, relevant, and time-bound objectives that can transform intentions into reality. Now it's time to see them in action. I've witnessed countless fathers move from feeling stuck to achieving real breakthrough moments, all by applying these principles we've discussed.

The power of SMART goals isn't in their complexity - it's in their simplicity. They take our biggest aspirations as fathers and break them down into clear, actionable steps. Instead of getting overwhelmed by the enormity of "becoming a better father," SMART goals give us a practical pathway forward.

Let me share three powerful examples that demonstrate exactly how other dads have put these principles to work. Their stories aren't just inspiring - they're practical blueprints you can adapt for your own fatherhood journey.

THREE FATHERS, THREE TRANSFORMATIONS

James's Story - From Missed Dinners to Meaningful Moments

James, a software developer and father of two, realized he was missing too many family dinners due to late work hours. Instead of making a vague promise to "be home more," he set a specific goal: to have dinner with his family four nights per week for the next three months. He measured this by tracking his attendance in a simple app and made it achievable by negotiating with his boss to leave work by 5:30 PM on designated days. The relevance was clear – his children were entering their teenage years, and these moments were precious. Within his three-month timeframe, James not only met his goal but discovered these regular dinners led to deeper conversations and stronger bonds with his kids.

Stephan's Story: Building Physical and Emotional Strength

After his divorce, Stephan struggled to maintain a strong connection with his 8-year-old son during their weekend visits. He created a SMART goal to spend 30 minutes every Saturday morning doing physical activities with his son for six months. He measured success through a shared fitness journal they maintained together. The goal was achievable because it required minimal equipment and could be done at local parks. It was relevant to both physical health and relationship building. By the end deadline, they had not only completed 24 workout sessions but had also developed a special ritual that gave them dedicated time to talk, laugh, and grow stronger together.

David's Story: From Financial Stress to Teaching Success

David worried about teaching his two children financial responsibility. Rather than just hoping they'd learn about money, he set a specific goal: to establish savings accounts for each child and teach them basic budgeting through weekly allowance management over four months. He measured progress by tracking their saving percentages and budget discussions. The goal was achievable through small weekly deposits and simple money lessons during Saturday morning breakfast. It was relevant to their future financial well-being and his role as a teacher and guide. By the target date, all three children had established saving habits and showed genuine interest in financial decisions, transforming David's anxiety into pride in their growing responsibility.

These stories share a common thread: each father transformed a general desire into concrete action through SMART goal-setting. They didn't just wish for better relationships with their children – they created specific, measurable plans and followed through. Their successes weren't just about meeting numerical targets; they were about building lasting habits that strengthened their roles as fathers and created deeper connections with their children.

MOVING FROM KNOWLEDGE TO ACTION

As I wrap up this chapter about bringing together all these pieces of Fathering Strong, I want you to remember something important: real change happens one small step at a time, just like how God led the Israelites through the wilderness - not in one giant leap, but day by day, with patience and purpose. The stories of James, Stephan, and David aren't just success stories - they're proof that any dad can create meaningful change when they combine clear goals with consistent action.

I'm excited to walk alongside you into our next chapter, "Tools for Transformation," where I'll share practical resources that have helped countless dads just like you. Think of it as your fatherhood toolkit - you'll get weekly planning templates that actually work for busy dads, goal-setting worksheets that make sense in the real world, and simple tracking tools that don't eat up your precious time. I'll even show you some great apps that can help keep you on track, family calendar ideas that really work, and thought-provoking questions that'll keep you focused on what truly matters.

These aren't just random worksheets I'm throwing at you - they're your bridge from "I want to be a better dad" to "I'm doing it!" Whether you're trying to get healthier, grow spiritually, or just spend more quality time with your kids, I've got something that'll help you make it happen. And don't worry - I'll show you how to handle the speed bumps along the way and adapt these tools to fit your unique situation.

Even the greatest cathedrals started with the right tools and a solid plan. Now, let's get you equipped to build something amazing - a legacy of strong fatherhood that'll impact generations to come.

CHAPTER 15

TOOLS FOR TRANSFORMATION - BUILDING THE FATHER YOU WANT TO BE

Let me tell you something I've learned on my own journey as a father: this calling we share isn't a quick dash to the finish line – it's a life-changing marathon. Just like the biblical principle of "running with perseverance the race marked out for us" (Hebrews 12:1), fatherhood is filled with moments that will take your breath away – those first wobbly steps, the pride of hearing "Dada," and yes, those nights when sleep feels like a distant memory. We've spent time in earlier chapters exploring why being an intentional father matters so deeply and how self-reflection and connection can transform your relationship with your kids. Now, I want to share with you the practical "how" – think of this chapter as your trusted toolbox, filled with resources you can reach for whether you're wrestling with bedtime battles or working to deepen those precious family bonds.

I get it – believe me. As fathers, we're constantly juggling what feels like a thousand spinning plates: work deadlines breathing down our necks, family commitments filling every calendar slot, and somewhere in there, trying to take care of ourselves too. That's exactly why I've designed these tools to be flexible and efficient. They're not about adding more to your already overflowing plate – they're about helping you make the most of the time you have, focusing on what truly matters in your journey as a dad.

CREATING YOUR VISION STATEMENT

Before we dive into the daily and weekly tools, let's start with something foundational – your fatherhood vision statement. Think of it as your North Star, guiding you through both the sunny days and storms of parenting. This isn't just some corporate exercise; it's about getting crystal clear on the father you want to become.

Take a moment to reflect on what being a father truly means to you. What qualities do you want your children to see in you? What values do you want to pass on? Your vision statement should capture both your aspirations and your commitments. For example, one father I worked with wrote: *"As a father, I strive to be patient, present, and nurturing for my children. Through my actions, I will demonstrate the values of integrity, compassion, and perseverance by modeling these behaviors in daily life and discussing their importance. Drawing from my experiences, I will build upon the positive aspects of family traditions and quality time while consciously avoiding criticism and emotional distance. My ultimate goal is to create a home where my children feel loved, secure, and empowered while helping them develop into confident, empathetic individuals who pursue their passions."*

You'll find a detailed worksheet in Appendix A to help you craft your own vision statement, which you can also download from www. fatheringstrongbook.com. Take your time with this – it's the foundation everything else will build upon.

SETTING AND PRIORITIZING YOUR SMART GOALS

With your vision statement as your compass, it's time to transform those aspirations into concrete action through SMART goals. These aren't just wishful thinking – they're Specific, Measurable, Achievable, Relevant, and Time-bound objectives that will guide your fatherhood journey.

I've created a comprehensive goal-setting worksheet in Appendix B (available at www.fatheringstrongbook.com) that helps you identify and prioritize your top fatherhood goals across the six key areas:

Physical Health: Your vitality and energy for active parenting

Spiritual Health: Your faith journey and spiritual leadership

Emotional Health: Your mental well-being and emotional intelligence

Financial Stewardship: Your family's financial security and teaching

Marriage Relationship: Your partnership with your children's mother

Child Relationships: Your individual bonds with each child

Take time to review each chapter in part 2 of this book again, noting the goals and action items that most strongly resonate with your vision statement. Look for patterns and themes that align with your core values and aspirations. Then, select 2-3 key goals from each area that you feel will have the greatest impact on your fatherhood journey. Remember, you don't need to tackle everything at once – focus on the goals that will move you closest to your vision while being realistic about your current season of life.

Once you've identified these initial goals, your next step is to narrow them down to your top 10 priorities. This focused approach prevents you from being overwhelmed and increases your likelihood of success. Review your list of goals (2-3 from each area) and evaluate each one based on its potential impact and alignment with your vision statement. Select the 10 goals that will create the most meaningful change in your fatherhood journey. These become your core focus areas – the foundational goals that will shape your action plans and drive your progress forward.

For each goal you set, you'll define three crucial elements:

> The deeper "why" behind the goal
> A specific target date for achievement
> Your immediate next action step

For instance, one father in our program set this SMART goal: "I will spend 30 minutes of focused, device-free time with each child every evening between 7-8 PM, starting this Monday." Notice how it hits all the SMART criteria while directly supporting his vision of being more present and engaged.

Keep these top 10 goals visible where you'll see them every day – maybe on your bathroom mirror, at your desk, or save as your phone's wallpaper. This constant reminder helps keep your priorities front and center as you navigate daily decisions and challenges. And here's something important to remember: these goals aren't set in stone. As your children grow and your family's needs evolve, your goals will naturally shift too. Don't get caught up trying to make them perfect from the start. What matters most is taking that first step, then the next, and the next. Each small action you take today – whether it's a five-minute conversation or a quick bedtime story – is actively shaping your children's tomorrow. Trust the process and keep moving forward.

THE WEEKLY PLANNING SYSTEM

Now here's where the rubber meets the road – your weekly planning system. Every Sunday evening (or whatever day/time works best for your schedule), take 15-20 minutes for what I call your Fathering Strong Weekly Plan. You'll find the complete template in Appendix C, available for download at www.fatheringstrongbook.com, but let me walk you through the key components.

Start by reviewing your vision statement and reflecting on the past week. What wins can you celebrate? What challenges did you face? What lessons did you learn? Then, choose one or two goals to focus on for the coming week. Be realistic – remember, we're running a marathon, not a sprint.

Plan specific quality time with each child. Maybe it's a Saturday morning bike ride with your daughter or helping your son with his science project. Block these times in your calendar just like you would an important meeting – because they are important meetings.

The weekly plan also includes sections for family activities, meal times together, and your spiritual focus. There's space to plan your self-care (because you can't pour from an empty cup) and to identify areas where you might need support or delegation.

THE DAILY DEVOTIONAL PRACTICE

If you're ready to take the next step and dive deeper into your daily spiritual journey, I've created the Fathering Strong Daily Devotional and Journal (template in Appendix D, downloadable from www. fatheringstrongbook.com.) This isn't just another task on your to-do list – it's your sacred space for connecting with God and reflecting on your fatherhood journey.

Each morning, you'll start with a Scripture reading and personal reflection. How does this passage speak to your role as a father? What wisdom can you apply today? There's space to record your gratitude, track your progress toward goals, and write specific prayers for your children, your growth as a father, and your family.

The emotional check-in section is particularly powerful. By acknowledging how you're feeling and understanding why, you can better manage how your emotions affect your parenting. One father shared how this practice helped him realize he was bringing work stress home and taking it out on his kids. That awareness led to positive changes in how he transitions from work to family time.

MAKING IT WORK IN REAL LIFE

Let me share something personal with you. During the COVID-19 lockdown, when I couldn't hug my kids or bounce my grandkids on my knee, my daily devotional became my lifeline. Every morning, I'd pour a cup of coffee, open my journal, and pour my heart out – all the worry, the love, the hopes I had for my family. It was in those quiet moments that I found the strength to get creative. Before I knew it, our weekly Zoom game nights became the highlight of our week.

I'm not the only one who's found power in this practice. Take Mike, a father of three teenagers. Through his daily journaling, he started noticing patterns in his kids' behaviors and his responses. Those insights led to breakthrough conversations with each child.

THE DIGITAL OPTION: USING DAY ONE

For those of you who prefer digital tools, I highly recommend the Day One app. Available on both iOS and Android, it's become my favorite journaling companion. The premium version ($35 annually) offers features like multiple journals, tags, and daily reminders that make it perfect for implementing our fatherhood system.

You can create separate journals for your daily devotions, prayer lists, and special moments with your kids. The ability to add photos, location data, and weather information helps create a rich record of your fatherhood journey. I've made our templates available at www.fatheringstrongbook. com, making it easy to start your digital journaling practice.

YOUR SUPPORT SYSTEM

Remember, you don't have to do this alone. Having an accountability partner is crucial for achieving your fatherhood goals. This could be another father, a mentor, or a close friend who shares your values. Schedule regular check-ins to review your progress, discuss challenges, and celebrate victories.

Consider joining a fathers' group at your church or starting one yourself. Better yet, join Fathering Strong to connect with dads who are walking the same path as you. There's incredible power in sharing your journey with other fathers who truly get it - the daily challenges, the small victories, and everything in between. Together, you can swap stories, learn from each other's wins and missteps, and build a supportive brotherhood that helps you become the dad you want to be.

CLOSING THOUGHTS

As we wrap up this chapter, I want you to remember something important: these tools are meant to serve you, not burden you. Start small. Maybe begin with just the weekly planning session, then gradually add the daily devotional. Or start with the digital journal and work your way up to the full system.

The goal isn't perfection – it's progress. Every step you take toward being more intentional in your fatherhood journey matters. Every prayer you write, every goal you set, every moment you spend in reflection is shaping not just your children's future, but your legacy as a father.

Remember what we talked about at the beginning of this book – being a father is one of the most important callings we'll ever receive. These tools are here to help you answer that calling with purpose, wisdom, and grace. They're designed to help you become not just a good father, but the father your children need you to be.

Take some time this week to start implementing these tools. Begin with your vision statement, then move on to setting your SMART goals. Choose an accountability partner and schedule your first weekly planning session. Take that first step, and trust that God will guide you on this journey of transformation.

Your children are worth every ounce of intention and effort you put into this journey. And you're not alone – you have these tools, this community, and most importantly, a heavenly Father who delights in helping His children become better fathers themselves.

CHAPTER 16

THE POWER OF THE FATHERING STRONG COMMUNITY

Being a father is one of life's greatest blessings - just as God designed it to be when He modeled perfect fatherhood for us. But man, some days it can feel like you're on an island all alone with your kids. When it seems like every parenting book and Facebook group is geared toward moms, it's easy to feel like you're flying solo on this journey. But here's the good news: you don't have to go it alone. There's a whole brotherhood of dads out there who get exactly what you're experiencing, and they're ready to lock arms with you.

In this chapter, I want to show you something game-changing - how plugging into the Fathering Strong community can transform your parenting journey. Whether you're still figuring out how to change diapers or you're a seasoned pro with teenagers, there's a place for you here. We're a group of regular guys who share one powerful mission: becoming the best dads we can be for our kids.

THE IMPORTANCE OF CONNECTION

Let me tell you something powerful: God created us for community. Just like the early church in Acts came together to support and encourage one another, we dads need that same kind of brotherhood. Think about it - when was the last time you had someone to high-five after your kid's first bike ride, or someone to text at midnight when you're struggling with a parenting decision?

That's exactly why having other dads in your corner is so crucial. When you're up at 3 AM with a colicky baby, knowing there's another dad out there who's been there (and survived!) can make all the difference. These connections aren't just nice to have - they're essential for thriving as a father.

And here's the beautiful thing: when you surround yourself with other dads who are passionate about being great fathers, it lights a fire under you too. You start picking up their wisdom, learning from their experiences, and before you know it, you're growing in ways you never expected. It's like having a personal coaching team for this whole dad thing!

Let me break down exactly how the Fathering Strong community works.

First, we have super active online forums. Think of them as your 24/7 dad hotline. Whether you're dealing with toddler tantrums or trying to figure out how to talk to your teenager about dating, there's always someone there who gets it.

We also have specialized groups for different dad situations - maybe you're a single dad, an adoptive father, or raising a child with special needs. Whatever your situation, we've got a crew of guys who understand exactly what you're walking through.

And if you're just starting out? Our mentorship program pairs you up with a dad who's been around the block a few times. Think of it as having a big brother in fatherhood who can show you the ropes.

We have also loaded up the community with resources to help you become a better father. Some of the many resources include:

> ▸ Expert articles that break down parenting challenges into practical steps

- ▸ Our weekly podcast featuring real dads sharing real stories
- ▸ Live webinars where you can learn from parenting experts
- ▸ A carefully curated book list (because who has time to read the bad ones?)
- ▸ Connections to local and national support services

The best part? All of this - the app, the resources, the whole community is completely free. We believe every dad deserves access to the support and tools they need to be their best.

Think of Fathering Strong as your backup team, your brain trust, your brotherhood in this amazing journey of fatherhood. We're here to celebrate your wins, help you through the tough spots, and remind you that you're not alone in this.

CHAPTER 17

LEAVING A LEGACY: THE IMPACT OF FATHERING STRONG

As we wrap up our journey together through the principles of Fathering Strong, I want to have a heart-to-heart with you about something that keeps me up at night: the legacy we're creating for our children. We've talked about virtues, goal-setting, and practical applications, but now let's focus on what God has truly called us to do as fathers – to leave an inheritance that matters eternally.

This isn't about the size of your bank account or achieving worldly success. As Proverbs 13:22 reminds us, "A good person leaves an inheritance for their children's children." I believe this inheritance goes far deeper than material wealth – it's about the spiritual and emotional riches we pass down through our daily actions, our steadfast love, and our living testimony of faith.

Let me share something with you. The other day, I was going through some old boxes and found a worn photograph of my dad. Looking at his weathered face, I was struck by how much of him I see in myself today. He wasn't one for lengthy sermons or emotional speeches, but he was a man that lived out his faith every day. He modeled Colossians 3:23 perfectly – working "as unto the Lord" in everything he did, whether he was staying up late to finish a work project or being the Scout Master of my Boy Scout troop. His quiet strength, unwavering integrity, and Christ-like servant's heart left an indelible mark on me and my sisters.

Even now, years after he's gone home to be with the Lord, his example continues to guide my steps as a father and grandfather.

That's what real legacy is about – living in such a way that the light of Christ shines through us and illuminates the path for generations to come.

BUILDING A LEGACY OF LOVE AND STRENGTH

What I've learned about leaving a legacy is it's not the big, dramatic moments that matter most – it's all those little day-to-day interactions that really shape who we become and what we pass on to our kids and grandkids.

Think about it this way. Every time you:

- Live out your values in front of your kids, showing them what honesty and integrity look like in real life
- Pick yourself up after a setback, dust yourself off, and try again – teaching them resilience without saying a word
- Stop what you're doing to really listen when they need to talk
- Show up consistently, whether it's for their little league games or helping with math homework
- Admit when you're wrong and ask for forgiveness – showing them what true humility looks like
- Choose to react with patience instead of anger

These aren't small choices - they're actually huge. They're the building blocks of your legacy, creating ripple effects that will influence not just your children, but generations to come. And here's the beautiful thing – you're already building this legacy, right now, in the everyday moments of being present with your family.

THE POWER OF SMALL MOMENTS

Let me share something that really brings this home. Years back, my son was terrified of heights – I mean, even a stepladder would make him freeze up. As I prayed about how to help him, I was reminded of Isaiah 41:13 "For I am the LORD your God who takes hold of your right hand and says to you, Do not fear; I will help you."

Just like God patiently guides us through our fears, I knew I needed to walk alongside my son through his. We started small – really small. I'd sit with him on the bottom step of the playground ladder, just talking and laughing. Some days we'd climb one rung higher, other days we'd stay put. But you know what? Those moments weren't really about conquering heights – they were about building trust, showing unconditional love.

Gradually, something beautiful unfolded. He not only conquered those physical heights but blossomed into a prolific rock wall climber in college. Those quiet moments of encouragement, our celebrations of tiny victories, the times I'd whisper "I believe in you" – they transformed into sacred spaces where God's love flowed through me to my son.

That's what I mean about legacy-building moments. They're in the bedtime prayers where we thank God for the day's adventures, in the Sunday morning pancake traditions where we talk about what we learned in church, in the tender moments when we process life's disappointments together. Each interaction is a chance to show our children what walking with God looks like in real life.

A CALL TO ACTION

This journey of Fathering Strong isn't some destination we arrive at – it's a beautiful, ongoing walk with God and our children. Just as Paul reminds us in Philippians 3:12, "Not that I have already obtained all this, or have already arrived at my goal, but I press on to take hold of that for which Christ Jesus took hold of me."

Every day brings new opportunities to grow, to learn, and to pour into our kids' lives. Sometimes we'll stumble, and that's okay.

Here's what I want you to take away from everything we've explored together: Let love be your compass. Just as our Heavenly Father's love guides and shapes us, let your love shape every interaction with your children – whether you're helping with homework, teaching them to ride a bike, or having those deep conversations about life's big questions.

This, my brothers, is how we build a legacy that matters. This is how we shape generations. This is how we become Fathering Strong.

EPILOGUE –
FATHERHOOD STORIES

Every father's journey tells a unique story of transformation, challenge, and growth. Throughout this book, we've explored over 85 stories from more than 20 fathers, each offering a window into the real-world challenges and triumphs of modern fatherhood. While each story carries its own wisdom, eight fathers' journeys stood out as particularly powerful testimonies to God's transformative work in families. Here, we take a deeper look at their stories—not because they're perfect fathers, but because their honest struggles and faithful persistence offer hope and practical wisdom for every dad seeking to lead his family with purpose.

To honor the privacy of the fathers who bravely shared their stories, all names have been changed throughout this book. While certain details have been modified to protect identities and better illustrate the principles being discussed, the heart of each story—the struggles, breakthroughs, and transformations—remains authentically true. These fathers trusted me with their vulnerable moments and profound revelations, and I have carefully preserved the essence of their experiences while ensuring their families' privacy.

MARK'S STORY: FROM SUCCESS TO SIGNIFICANCE

Mark's journey as a father began with a devastating fire that destroyed his family's home. In that moment of loss, they discovered something profound in Psalm 32:7, "You are my hiding place; you will protect me from trouble and surround me with songs of deliverance." What seemed like tragedy became a turning point in Mark's fatherhood story.

As a high-powered executive, Mark had always equated stress with success. His children received what little energy remained after long days at the office. But through the fire's aftermath, he learned that true security—and true fatherhood—wasn't built on material success or professional achievement. It was founded on something far more lasting: God's faithful presence.

The transformation began with small steps. Mark started each day with prayer and Scripture instead of emails. He created a "Shield Wall" in their new home—a prayer space where the family could openly share their challenges and face them together in faith. During lunch breaks, he took short walks to pray and reflect, gradually learning to carry his burdens differently, with God's guidance.

Perhaps Mark's most powerful moment as a father came when he apologized to his daughter after losing his temper. "It was hard admitting I was wrong," he shared with our father's group, his voice thick with emotion, "but showing her that even fathers make mistakes – that felt like real strength."

Today, Mark leads his family with a different kind of strength. He and his wife Julie practice intentional connection, from their 20-second morning hugs to their "curiosity conversations" at dinner. They've transformed their approach to family finances through biblical principles, and their home resonates with deep discussions that teach their children to think critically and spiritually.

Mark's story reminds us that great fathers aren't born—they're forged through challenges, humility, and a willingness to grow. His journey from career-focused executive to spiritually grounded dad offers hope and practical wisdom for every father seeking to lead his family with purpose and grace.

PETER'S STORY: THE POWER OF SMALL CHANGES

While Mark's story shows how crisis can catalyze transformation, Peter's journey demonstrates how small, faithful changes can reshape a family's entire dynamic. Once quick-tempered and distant, he learned to pause and pray instead of yelling when frustrated with his children. His vulnerability became a powerful teaching tool - his seven-year-old daughter even reminded him during a stressful moment, "Daddy, remember what you taught us - we can tell God anything." These moments of gentle accountability from his children became precious signs of God's work in their family.

As a father of four, Peter faced many challenges that tested his faith and character. When God called him to increase his giving despite job uncertainty, he and his wife stepped out in faith with their tithe. Their trust paid off - not just through an unexpected promotion, but in watching their teenage sons develop wisdom about money. The boys began saving portions of their allowances for church missions and local charities, following their parents' example of faithful stewardship.

Through fifteen years of marriage, Peter and Sarah weathered various storms by anchoring themselves in Scripture and daily practices that strengthened their family. They started morning prayer times, evening "heart talks," and connection rituals like sharing "high-low" moments at dinner. These simple but consistent habits formed their family's spiritual backbone. Even during busy seasons or vacations, they kept these touchpoints, knowing their children thrived on the stability.

Peter's biggest growth came in how he communicated. "I was always interrupting Sarah, trying to fix everything instead of just listening," he admits. Guided by James 1:19, he became quick to listen and slow to speak. This change not only deepened his marriage but caught their teenage daughter's attention. She later shared that watching her parents work through conflicts with grace helped her handle her own friendship challenges at school.

The journey had its setbacks. Peter sometimes fell back into old patterns, especially during stressful work periods or financial pressure. But these struggles became opportunities for the family to witness genuine repentance and restoration. His children learned that spiritual growth isn't about perfection but about persistent trust in God's transforming power.

Today, Peter and Sarah's home demonstrates what happens when a father commits to spiritual growth and authentic relationships. Their story shows that fatherhood isn't about perfection, but about taking consistent, faithful steps toward becoming the father God calls us to be. Their example has inspired other families in their church to pursue intentional spiritual practices, creating a ripple effect throughout their congregation.

Their transformation reaches beyond their immediate family. Peter now mentors younger fathers, sharing his successes and failures with humility. Sarah leads a women's group focused on building strong family foundations, drawing from their shared journey of growth and grace. Together, they've found that God's faithfulness in their family story has equipped them to encourage others on similar paths.

TOM'S JOURNEY: FINDING STRENGTH IN ADVERSITY

If Peter's story illustrates the impact of gradual change, Tom's narrative reveals how faith can sustain us through life's most challenging seasons. As a single dad of three, he faced challenges that would test any parent's resolve: job loss during the pandemic, a bitter divorce, mounting debt, and his son's medical crisis. Yet each challenge revealed new depths of his character and resilience.

When the pandemic claimed his job, Tom transformed his garage into a custom furniture workshop, showing his children how to turn adversity into opportunity. During his divorce, he chose love over bitterness, letting his faith guide him through the storm. When medical bills threatened to overwhelm his family after his son's surgery, he faced the challenge head-on, negotiating payment plans and finding solutions rather than surrendering to despair.

Perhaps most touching was his journey to connect with his teenage daughter. Moving beyond quick answers and distracted conversations, Tom learned the art of genuine listening. Their shared discovery of his passion for architecture became a bridge between their worlds, leading to deeper discussions about life, faith, and dreams.

Today, Tom's story stands as a beacon of hope for other fathers. He's not just surviving but thriving - running a successful business, debt-free, and maintaining strong relationships with all three of his children. His journey reminds us that fatherhood isn't about perfection; it's about persistence, growth, and the courage to face each new challenge with unwavering love and determination.

Through every storm and victory, Tom has demonstrated that the heart of fatherhood lies not in avoiding life's challenges, but in showing our children how to face them with grace, faith, and resilience.

MIKE'S JOURNEY: BREAKING GENERATIONAL PATTERNS

While Tom's story demonstrates resilience through external challenges, Mike's journey reveals the power of healing internal wounds. Growing up without a dad left him feeling adrift when it came to raising his own three children. "I had no blueprint," he often admits with a mix of vulnerability and hard-earned wisdom. But through his faith journey and participation in Fathering Strong, Mike discovered that God would become the Father he never had—and the model for the father he wanted to be.

Today, Mike and his wife Jenny parent their three teenagers with intention and grace. Their home radiates the principles of biblical fatherhood: from teaching financial stewardship through first fruits giving, to setting loving boundaries, to modeling a Christ-centered marriage. Their evening "sacred hour"—free from phones and distractions—has transformed their relationship and shown their children what genuine partnership looks like. It's become such a cherished tradition that even their busy teenagers prioritize this family time, knowing it's non-negotiable but also deeply meaningful.

Mike's greatest joy comes from seeing how his intentional fathering impacts his children. His daughter's gratitude for firm boundaries, his son's vulnerable conversations during their weekend runs, and his youngest's observation of her parents' loving marriage all testify to the power of present, purposeful fatherhood. Each small victory—whether it's a heartfelt conversation about faith or watching his children make wise choices—reminds Mike that breaking generational patterns is possible through God's guidance.

"When I stopped trying to have all the answers and started leading with authenticity," Mike reflects, "everything changed. God didn't just show me how to be a father—He showed me how to be His child first." This revelation transformed not only his parenting but his entire approach to life and leadership within his family.

Through daily journaling, active participation in father's groups, and a commitment to growing in his faith, Mike continues to build the legacy he never inherited. He's expanded his influence beyond his immediate family, mentoring other fathers who, like him, want to break free from the constraints of their past. Every Wednesday morning, you'll find him at the local coffee shop, sharing his experiences with younger dads who are just beginning their parenting journey.

His story reminds us that with God as our model, any father can become the dad their children need. Mike's journey from fatherless son to faithful father serves as a powerful testimony to God's redemptive work in families. "It's not about being perfect," he often tells the men he mentors, "it's about being present, being purposeful, and being led by God's perfect love."

JAMES'S STORY: REDEFINING SUCCESS

Mike's journey from growing up without a father to becoming a devoted dad himself sets the stage for James's powerful story of redefining success. Once a workaholic executive who spent 70 hours a week at his software development firm, James realized that real success meant being there for his children, Sarah (14) and Michael (16). His Sunday afternoon walks with Sarah created a special space where she felt comfortable opening up about her life. Meanwhile, his honest talks with Michael about challenging topics like mental health and cyberbullying have built a deeper connection than he ever thought possible. These seemingly simple moments have woven themselves into precious memories that both children cherish.

After Michael's severe mental health crisis five years ago, James completely changed his approach to fatherhood. The crisis showed him that corporate success meant nothing if his home life was falling apart. He switched to flexible hours, made weekly family dinners mandatory, and became a leading voice for online safety at his children's schools. His marriage to Rachel had suffered from his constant absence, but their shared focus on biblical money management and regular counseling sessions brought them closer. They learned that time invested in their relationship paid off more than any financial investment could.

Making these changes wasn't simple. James weathered doubt from his coworkers and battled guilt about scaling back his work hours. But seeing positive changes in his kids proved he'd made the right call. Sarah grew more confident with her dad around more, while Michael's grades and emotional health improved significantly. Their slower-paced family life created room for real connections and meaningful talks that their previous hectic schedule never allowed.

His journey shows that it's never too late to change direction, and that our biggest parenting struggles often teach us the most about leadership. "Every day, I'm learning," James reflects. "And every day, I'm grateful for second chances."

James's transformation has created lasting waves of change. His software company now offers more family-friendly policies, and several fellow executives have started prioritizing family time too. Through everything, James maintains that his greatest success isn't his thriving business or community impact, but seeing his children's genuine smiles when he comes home each evening.

DAVID'S STORY: FINDING PURPOSE THROUGH PAIN

While James learned to balance career and family, David's story shows how personal tragedy can become a platform for helping others. After losing his wife to cancer, this single father of two, including his son Noah who has autism, transformed his deepest challenges into opportunities to serve others. What began as a personal journey of advocating for Noah's educational needs evolved into creating an inclusive support program at their local school district that benefits countless families today.

As the founder of a parent support group for families navigating autism and special needs, David helps other parents discover their own courage and resilience. His "First Things First" morning routine system, born from his desire to bring order to family chaos, has been adopted by many families in his community.

By day, David works two jobs to support his family and fund specialized treatments for Noah. By night, he's a dedicated father who believes in the power of showing up - whether that's for his daughter's dance recitals, his children's homework sessions, or his weekly volunteer work at the local hospice center where his late wife spent her final days.

David often says his greatest achievement isn't in the programs he's created or the battles he's won, but in teaching his children that true strength comes through vulnerability and faith. His story reminds us that fatherhood isn't about having all the answers, but about being willing to search for them, one step at a time. His journey from an overwhelmed father to a community leader exemplifies how love, determination, and faith can transform life's greatest challenges into opportunities for growth and service.

CARLOS'S STORY: BUILDING A LEGACY OF FAITH

David's commitment to serving others finds a parallel in Carlos's dedication to building a spiritual legacy. Having emigrated from his homeland twenty-five years ago with little more than dreams and determination, Carlos's journey demonstrates how faith can transform not just a family, but generations. Through long nights of uncertainty and days of grueling work, his vision of creating a better life for his future family never wavered. Today, he and his wife lead a vibrant household of four children in a home where faith forms their foundation. Each morning begins as it has for decades—with the family gathered in prayer, weaving a spiritual legacy into his children's lives.

Having grown up with an angry father, Carlos struggled with his own anger until he encountered 1 Corinthians 13:4-7 in a men's group: "Love is patient, love is kind. It does not envy, it does not boast, it is not proud. It does not dishonor others, it is not self-seeking, it is not easily angered, it keeps no record of wrongs..." These words struck deep, challenging his patterns of behavior. He began measuring his actions against this scripture daily, asking himself, "Was I patient with Maria today? Kind?" His children noticed the change in his demeanor and began approaching him more freely, without their previous hesitation.

Committed to change, Carlos attended anger management classes for six months, learning to breathe through frustration and communicate with his teenage son patiently. Though the classes forced him to confront uncomfortable truths about himself and his parenting, his persistence paid off—his son now seeks his counsel instead of avoiding him. Through a Dad's group on Fathering Strong, Carlos also learned to bring godly order to what he jokingly called "chaos," where bedtimes, meals, and homework lacked structure. He established consistent routines that gave his children stability while preserving their home's warm, loving atmosphere.

Now, Carlos creates intentional moments of connection, sitting with his teenage son each evening, phones set aside, simply listening. "Most nights he barely says a word," Carlos shares, "but when he needs to talk, he knows I'm there." These quiet moments have become sacred spaces where trust grows and understanding deepens. His wife Maria sees the profound change in their family dynamics, noting, "Carlos has become the spiritual anchor our children need in these challenging times."

His journey from immigrant to exemplary father embodies the timeless principles of dedication, sacrifice, and spiritual leadership explored throughout this book. The transformation demanded countless moments of self-reflection, prayer, and conscious choice to break old patterns. Through Carlos's story, we see how unwavering faith and intentional parenting can shape not just a family, but generations to come. His example inspires other fathers seeking to create lasting, positive change in their families, proving that with God's guidance and determined effort, any man can become the father his children need.

ALEX'S STORY: EMBRACING LIFE'S CHALLENGES

Our final story brings together many themes we've explored—from facing unexpected diagnoses to managing financial challenges. Alex's journey embodies the challenges of modern fatherhood, particularly through raising a son with autism. Through this experience, he discovered how faith could transform seemingly insurmountable obstacles into opportunities for growth. "Faith gave me patience I didn't know I had," he shares, a lesson that shaped his approach to both parenting and mentoring other fathers of children with special needs. While the diagnosis initially overwhelmed him, prayer and community support helped Alex learn to celebrate his son's unique perspective on the world.

After marrying Lisa and leaving his parents' home, Alex faced the delicate balance of honoring his original family while building his own. He found guidance in scripture, particularly Genesis 2:24, which helped him understand this transition as part of God's natural design for families. This transition wasn't always smooth - cultural expectations and family traditions sometimes clashed with the couple's vision for their new life together. Through open communication and mutual respect, they found ways to blend the best of both worlds.

Now a father of two, he implements creative parenting strategies like the "Integrity Stars" system to reinforce family values, while maintaining monthly check-ins with his wife to ensure their family stays aligned. The Integrity Stars system, which rewards children for demonstrating core values like honesty, kindness, and responsibility, has become a model for other families in their church community. These regular check-ins with Lisa have proven crucial in maintaining unity in their parenting approach and strengthening their marriage.

Despite carrying $80,000 in student loan debt early in his journey, Alex demonstrated remarkable financial stewardship through careful planning, strict budgeting, and strategic career moves. He and Lisa lived frugally, cooking at home, shopping at thrift stores, and finding free family activities in their community. Their dedication to financial responsibility allowed them to become debt-free within five years, an achievement that Alex now uses to encourage other young families struggling with similar financial burdens.

Today, he mentors other fathers, sharing both practical wisdom and spiritual insights gained from his experiences. His weekly men's group at church has become a safe haven for fathers facing similar challenges, where they can openly discuss their struggles and victories. Alex's approach combines biblical principles with practical applications, helping fathers develop both their spiritual leadership and practical parenting skills.

His story reminds us that fatherhood, with all its challenges, offers unprecedented opportunities for personal growth, deeper faith, and meaningful impact on others. Through his example, Alex shows that the journey of fatherhood, while often difficult, can become a powerful testimony of God's grace and guidance in our lives. His experience continues to inspire other fathers to embrace their role with courage, wisdom, and unwavering faith.

APPENDIX A - FATHERING STRONG VISION WORKSHEET

Creating a clear vision for your fatherhood journey is the essential first step before setting specific goals. This vision serves as your North Star, providing direction and purpose that will guide all your parenting decisions and actions. Just as a builder needs blueprints before construction, a father needs a well-defined vision before developing SMART goals and action plans. This vision will help you stay focused on what truly matters, deepen your connection with your children, and transform your aspirations into reality. Use this worksheet to reflect deeply on your values, define your purpose, and craft a compelling vision that will guide you on your path to becoming a Fathering Strong dad.

1. Reflect on Your Role as a Father

a. What does being a father mean to you? Think beyond daily tasks to understand your deeper purpose as a father List your top 3 things.

1.

2.

3.

b. What kind of father do you want your children to see? Consider the qualities you demonstrate that you hope your children will naturally embrace. List the top 3 qualities.

1.

2.

3.

c. What three words best describe the father you aspire to be?

1.

2.

3

2. Identify Your Core Values

a. What key values do you want to pass on to your children? (e.g., kindness, honesty, responsibility, faith). List your top 3,

1.

2.

3.

b. How will you demonstrate these values in your daily life? Identify one way for each of the 3 values you identified.

1.

2.

3.

3. How do your experiences with your father (or father figures) shape your vision?

Consider both the positive lessons and the gaps in your upbringing. Add your top 3 positive and top 3 negative. If you don't have that many in either category, just list as many (or any) that you remember.

Positive experiences:

1.

2.

3.

Negative experiences:

1.

2.

3.

COMPLETE YOUR VISION STATEMENT AS A FATHER

Using your reflections above, write a brief vision statement that captures your commitment to fatherhood. This should inspire and motivate you daily. You can fill in the blanks of the provided template if that helps.

As a father, I strive to be _____, _____, and _____ (three aspirational qualities) for my children. Through my actions, I will demonstrate the values of _____, _____, and _____ (your core values) by _____ (specific ways you'll show these values). Drawing from my experiences, I will build upon the positive aspects of _____ (positive experiences) while consciously avoiding _____ (negative experiences). My ultimate goal is to create a home where my children feel _____, _____, and _____ (desired environment/feelings for your children) while helping them develop into _____ (type of people you hope they become).

Example Vision Statements Using Template:

"As a father, I strive to be patient, present, and nurturing for my children. Through my actions, I will demonstrate the values of integrity, compassion, and perseverance by modeling these behaviors in daily life and discussing their importance. Drawing from my experiences, I will build upon the positive aspects of family traditions and quality time while consciously avoiding criticism and emotional distance. My ultimate goal is to create a home where my children feel loved, secure, and empowered while helping them develop into confident, empathetic individuals who pursue their passions."

"As a father, I strive to be consistent, encouraging, and wise for my children. Through my actions, I will demonstrate the values of honesty, responsibility, and kindness by teaching through example and celebrating their efforts. Drawing from my experiences, I will build upon the positive aspects of open communication and unconditional support while consciously avoiding harsh judgment and unrealistic expectations. My ultimate goal is to create a home where my children feel accepted, inspired, and understood while helping them develop into resilient, compassionate leaders."

"As a father, I strive to be supportive, authentic, and dependable for my children. Through my actions, I will demonstrate the values of respect, curiosity, and determination by actively engaging in their interests and showing genuine care. Drawing from my experiences, I will build upon the positive aspects of shared adventures and meaningful conversations while consciously avoiding emotional unavailability and inconsistency. My ultimate goal is to create a home where my children feel valued, safe, and confident while helping them develop into independent, well-rounded individuals who make positive contributions to their community."

For a printable copy of the Fathering Strong 30-day Daily Devotional and Journal Vision worksheet and to order a copy of the printed journal go to www.fatheringstrongbook.com.

APPENDIX B - SMART GOAL BLUEPRINT SUMMARY WORKSHEET

STEP 1: YOUR VISION STATEMENT

[Copy your vision statement from Appendix A here]

STEP 2: REVIEW OF SMART GOALS FOR EACH KEY AREA

Take time to review each chapter and identify your SMART goals. Compare them with your vision statement and select the goals that best align with the future father you want to become. Write these goals in the sections below, grouping them by key area.

As you review each goal, ask yourself:

- › Is it Specific? (Clear and well-defined)
- › Is it Measurable? (Has concrete success criteria)
- › Is it Achievable? (Realistic within your circumstances)
- › Is it Relevant? (Directly supports your vision)
- › Is it Time-bound? (Has a clear deadline)

Refine any goals that don't fully meet these criteria. For example, change "Be more present with my kids" to "Spend 30 minutes of undistracted playtime with each child every evening." This focused approach will help you build a roadmap of meaningful goals that truly support your vision of fatherhood.

1. Physical Health

> Physical Fitness
> Nutrition
> Relaxation

2. Spiritual Health

> Prayer
> Bible Study
> Community of Fathers

3. Emotional Health

> Stress Management
> Vulnerability
> Communications

4. Financial Wealth

> Budgeting
> Saving and Investing
> Stewardship
> Debt Management

5. Marriage Relationship

> Communications
> Intimacy
> Shared Values
> Quality Time

6. Child Relationships

> ➤ Core Values
> ➤ Communication
> ➤ Quality Time
> ➤ Discipline

STEP 3: GOAL PRIORITY LIST

Review all the goals you've identified and select your top ten most important goals. Rank them below, with #1 being your highest priority. For each goal, include:

> ➤ The specific goal
> ➤ Why it matters to you and your children
> ➤ Your target date for achieving it
> ➤ First action step to take

Priority #1
Goal:
Why it matters:
Target Date:
First Action:

Priority #2
Goal:
Why it matters:
Target Date:
First Action:

Priority #3
Goal:
Why it matters:
Target Date:
First Action:

Priority #4
Goal:
Why it matters:
Target Date:
First Action:

Priority #5
Goal:
Why it matters:
Target Date:
First Action:

Priority #6
Goal:
Why it matters:
Target Date:
First Action:

Priority #7
Goal:
Why it matters:
Target Date:
First Action:

Priority #8
Goal:
Why it matters:
Target Date:
First Action:

Priority #9
Goal:
Why it matters:
Target Date:
First Action:

Priority #10
Goal:
Why it matters:
Target Date:
First Action:

MONTHLY REVIEW

Schedule time at the end of each month to review your progress:

Review Date:

Goals achieved:

Goals in progress:

Goals needing adjustment

New insights or lessons learned:

ACCOUNTABILITY PARTNER

Having an accountability partner is crucial for achieving your fatherhood goals. This trusted individual will help keep you on track, provide honest feedback, and celebrate your successes along the way. Regular check-ins with your accountability partner create a structure for reviewing progress and addressing challenges. Choose someone who understands your vision of fatherhood and isn't afraid to have difficult conversations when needed. This could be a fellow father, mentor, or close friend who shares your values and commitment to personal growth. Your accountability partner will help ensure you're staying true to your vision statement and making consistent progress toward becoming the father you aspire to be.

Name:

Contact information:

Check-in frequency:

Next scheduled check-in:

Remember: Your goals should align with your vision statement and reflect the father you want to become. Review and adjust these priorities regularly as your children grow and circumstances change. Keep this worksheet visible and refer to it daily to stay focused on your fatherhood journey.

For a printable copy of the Fathering Strong 30-day Daily Devotional and Journal Blueprint Summary worksheet and to order a copy of the printed journal go to www.fatheringstrongbook.com

APPENDIX C - FATHERING STRONG WEEKLY CHECK-IN PLAN WORKSHEET

TIPS FOR USING THIS WORKSHEET

Start your planning session with prayer and reflection. Take time to truly consider each section rather than rushing through. Keep this plan visible - perhaps in your workspace or on your phone - for daily reference. Share relevant portions with your spouse to ensure alignment in parenting goals. Remember that flexibility is key - unexpected moments often provide the best opportunities for connection with your children.

Review this plan each Sunday evening to prepare for the week ahead. Consider it a living document that evolves with your family's needs and growth. The goal isn't perfection but progress in becoming more intentional in your role as a father.

This template serves as your weekly compass, helping you navigate the beautiful journey of fatherhood with purpose and grace. Use it as a tool to transform your fatherhood vision into daily actions that will shape your children's lives and leave a lasting legacy of love, wisdom, and faith.

Remember that this template is just a starting point - a framework to help guide your intentional fatherhood journey. Not every section may apply to your specific situation, and that's perfectly fine. Feel free to modify, adapt, or skip sections based on what resonates most with your family's needs and circumstances. The key is to use this template in a way that authentically supports your growth as a father, rather than feeling pressured to fill in every blank. Make it your own, and let it evolve alongside your fatherhood journey.

WEEKLY VISION CHECK-IN

Take a moment to review your vision statement and reflect on how this week's activities align with becoming the father you aspire to be.

Vision Statement Review Space:

LAST WEEK'S REFLECTION

Celebrating Wins (Both big and small victories with your children):

Challenges Faced:

Lessons Learned:

THIS WEEK'S FOCUS

Primary Goal for the Week:

Why this goal matters to my children:

Specific actions I will take:

QUALITY TIME PLANNING

One-on-One Time (Plan individual time with each child):

Child's Name:
Activity:
When:

Child's Name:
Activity:
When:

FAMILY CONNECTION

Family Activity Plan:

Meal Times Together:

Faith/Spiritual Focus:

SELF-CARE & GROWTH

Personal Development Focus:

Physical Health Plan:

Spiritual Practice:

RESOURCE MANAGEMENT

Areas to Delegate:

Areas to Simplify:

Areas to Stop:

WEEKLY PRAYER

Specific prayers for each child:

Family prayer focus:

Personal growth prayer:

NOTES & IDEAS

Space for additional thoughts, inspirations, or reminders:

Signature:
Date:

Remember: This plan is a living document. Adjust it as needed while keeping your vision of intentional fatherhood at the center. Review it daily, preferably during your morning routine, to stay focused on what matters most - being the father your children need.

For a printable copy of the Fathering Strong 30-day Daily Devotional and Journal Weekly Check-in Plan worksheet and to order a copy of the printed journal go to www.fatheringstrongbook.com.

APPENDIX D - DAILY DEVOTIONAL AND JOURNAL TEMPLATE

SCRIPTURE AND REFLECTION

Today's Date:

Scripture Reading:

FATHERING STRONG FOCUS

Core strength and virtue:

Today's Quote:

Fatherhood Daily Tip:

SCRIPTURE FOCUS

Scripture for today:

How the scripture applies to my role as a father:

PERSONAL REFLECTION SPACE

The progress I made yesterday toward my goals

The one thing I learned about myself yesterday

Blessings I noticed yesterda

EMOTIONAL CHECK-IN

Today I Feel:

Why I Feel This Way:

How These Emotions Affected My Parenting:

DAILY ACTION STEPS

Today's primary goal and action I will take:

Today's actions that address the four virtues (courage, fortitude, faith and love):

PRAYER FOCUS

Prayers for my growth as a father:

Prayers for my children:

Prayers for my marriage/family:

Other Prayers:

Remember: This journal is your sacred space for honest reflection and spiritual growth. Use it to track your journey, celebrate progress, and stay focused on becoming the father God has called you to be. Feel free to adapt this template to better serve your needs and circumstances.

For a printable copy of the Fathering Strong 30-day Daily Devotional and Journal daily worksheet and to order a copy of the printed journal go to www.fatheringstrongbook.com.

ABOUT THE AUTHOR

Bruce Stapleton combines corporate leadership, entrepreneurial success, and deep spiritual commitment in his work on Biblical fatherhood. His expertise comes from over 25 years of creating and teaching Christian adult education in parenting, alongside his hands-on leadership of fatherhood initiatives through Urban Light Ministries. As a program leader of the Fathering Strong program and former Board Chairman working with founder and President Pastor Eli Williams, Bruce has gained deep insight into modern fathers' challenges and the Biblical solutions that can transform their families.

His innovative support for fathers shines through in the co-development of the "Fathering Strong" app, delivering daily inspiration and practical, Bible-based advice. Through his leadership of the Fathering Strong podcast and management of Urban Light Ministries' digital presence, Bruce has become a trusted voice in faith-based fatherhood education.

Bruce's corporate experience includes executive positions at NCR Corporation, where he led worldwide services marketing and strategic planning. His entrepreneurial spirit led him to create the award-winning Lifegevity program in preventive health and wellness, showing his talent for developing practical life solutions. As a current college digital marketing instructor with both a Bachelor's in Business and Economics and an MBA, he brings both academic knowledge and real-world experience to his fatherhood teachings.

Bruce's perspective is uniquely shaped by his role as a father of four and grandfather of four, along with his appreciation for positive male role models across generations. His father and grandfather taught him traditional skills like woodworking and outdoor activities, experiences that have informed his understanding of how fathers can build lasting connections with their children. His 42-year marriage and active church ministry involvement strengthen his authority in teaching Biblical fatherhood principles.

Readers find in Bruce's work an exceptional blend of practical experience, professional expertise, and spiritual wisdom. He bridges the gap between Biblical teachings and modern parenting challenges, offering fathers a clear path to building stronger, faith-centered families. Through his writing, Bruce delivers both the inspiration and practical tools fathers need to positively impact their children's lives and their communities.

BIBLICAL REFERENCE

All Scripture quotations and references, unless otherwise indicated, are taken from the New International Version (NIV) Bible reference at www.biblegateway.com.

1 Chronicles 23:28-32 12

1 Chronicles 29:14 115

1 Corinthians 9:24-27 77

1 Corinthians 13:4-7 131

1 Corinthians 14:33 . . . . 12, 146

1 Corinthians 16:13-14 4

1 Corinthians 16:14 42

1 John 3:18 91

1 John 4:18 45

1 John 4:19 93

1 Kings 17:2-6, ... 14

1 Peter 3 131

1 Peter 4:10 120

1 Thessalonians 5:17 82

1 Timothy 6:17 116

2 Corinthians 6:18 xii

2 Corinthians 9:7 114

2 Corinthians 9:11 93

2 Corinthians 12:9-10 104

2 Peter 1:3 15

2 Samuel 22:47 16

2 Timothy 1:5 169

2 Timothy 1:7 30

2 Timothy 3:16-17 83

Acts 2:42 88

Colossians 2:5 12

Colossians 3:12 93

Colossians 3:23 191

Colossians 4:6 134

Daniel 6:10 17

Daniel 6:26-27 17

Deuteronomy 6:6-7 . . . . 93, 146

Deuteronomy 6:7 . . . . 138, 151

Deuteronomy 11:19 80

Deuteronomy 32:4 16

Ecclesiastes 3:1 102

Ecclesiastes 4:9-10 . . . . 86, 172

Ecclesiastes 4:12 77

Ecclesiastes 5:10 114

Ephesians 1:3 15

Ephesians 3:14-15 170

Ephesians 3:17-19 46

Ephesians 4:15 . . . . 108, 133

Ephesians 5:21-33 131

Ephesians 5:25-33 83

Ephesians 6:4 . . . . 4, 39, 83, 162

Ephesians 6:10 21

Ephesians 6:10-18 . . . . 7, 18, 76

Ephesians 6:14 19

Ephesians 6:15 19

Ephesians 6:16 . . . . 9, 19

Ephesians 6:16-17 20

Ephesians 6:17 20

Exodus 18:17-23 . . . . 12, 146

Galatians 5:22-23 . . . . .90, 97

Galatians 6:1 163

Galatians 6:2 89

Genesis 1 11

Genesis 2:24 . . . . .130, 205

Hebrews 4:12 85

Hebrews 10:24-25 87

Hebrews 12:1 181

Hebrews 12:6 163

Hebrews 13:8 17

Isaiah 26:4 18

Isaiah 41:10 10

Isaiah 41:13 193

James 1:5 . . . . 15, 83, 116

James 1:17 . . . . 16, 17

James 1:19. 90, 98, 108, 133, 155, 197

James 1:22 . . . . .xii, 77

James 2:17 89

James 4:8 169

James 5:13 80

James 5:16 87

Jeremiah 33:3 78

Jeremiah 33:25-26 12

Job 1:5 146

Job 13:15 33

Job 38:33 12

John 1:17 163

John 13:14-15 91

John 14:27 101

Joshua 1:9 . . . . .4, 32, 126

Joshua 24:15 . . . . .78, 137

Luke 5:16 78

Luke 14:28 114

Luke 18 33

Malachi 3:10 14

Mark 6:31 101

Matthew 5:16 90

Matthew 6:6 80

Matthew 6:11 15

Matthew 6:21 97

Matthew 6:24 112

Matthew 6:26 13

Matthew 6:31-33 116

Matthew 6:33 118

Matthew 7:9-11 146

Matthew 7:24-27 . . . . 17, 76

Matthew 11:28 . . . . .68, 103

Matthew 18:15-17 83

Matthew 19:6 131

Matthew 19:26 96

Matthew 25:14-30 . . . . 113, 119

Matthew 25:40 . . . . .78, 93

Philippians 1:6 96

Philippians 3:12 193

Philippians 4:6-7 81

Philippians 4:8 100

Philippians 4:11 117

Philippians 4:11-13 17

Philippians 4:13 . . . . .34, 172

Philippians 4:19 . . . .15, 112, 126, 146

Proverbs 2:6-7 15

Proverbs 3:6 13

Proverbs 3:9 116

Proverbs 3:9-10 14

Proverbs 4:1-6 146

Proverbs 4:23 97

Proverbs 9:10 28

Proverbs 10:25 18

Proverbs 13:22 . . . . 120, 139, 191

Proverbs 13:24 163

Proverbs 14:8 116

Proverbs 15:1 . . . . .99, 108

Proverbs 16:9 . . . . 169, 171

Proverbs 16:32 111

Proverbs 18:21 . . . . 109, 133

Proverbs 18:22 141

Proverbs 21:5 . . . . .94, 113, 128

Proverbs 21:20 . . . . 113, 116, 119

Proverbs 22:6 163

Proverbs 22:7 . . . . .83, 113, 122

Proverbs 22:26 123
Proverbs 24:16 22
Proverbs 27:12 123
Proverbs 27:17 85
Proverbs 27:23 115
Psalm 18:2 . . . . 18, 146
Psalm 18:30 9
Psalm 19:7-9 12
Psalm 32:7 . . . . 10, 195
Psalm 34:10 15
Psalm 34:17 81
Psalm 34:19 33
Psalm 37:21 123
Psalm 46:1 76
Psalm 56:3 17

Psalm 62:2: 16
Psalm 91:4 8
Psalm 103:13 . . . . 4, 39
Psalm 104:19 12
Psalm 121:7-8 9
Psalm 127:1 16
Psalm 128:3 144
Psalm 139:14 90
Romans 4:3 27
Romans 5:3-4 126
Romans 8:6 102
Romans 12:18 83
Song of Solomon 8:6 135
Titus 1:5 12
Zechariah 4:10 126

WORKS CITED

Calm. n.d. *Calm.com*. Accessed April 10, 2022. https://www.calm.com/.

2008. *Fireproof*. Directed by Alex Kendrick. Performed by Kirk Cameron.

Cargal, Timothy, Mark Chavalas, and James R.: et. al. Edwards. 2014. *Chronological Study Bible*. Nashville, TN: Thomas Nelson.

Cronometer. n.d. *Cronometer*. Accessed January 18, 2025. https://cronometer.com/.

Earle, Richard. 1989. *Your Vitality Quotient: The Clinically Proven Program That Can Reduce Your Body Age*. Toronto, Canada: Grand Central Publishing.

Egan, John and Strohm, Mitch. 2021. *The Debt Avalanche Method: How it Works and How to Use It*. July 30. Accessed December 18, 2024. https://www.forbes.com/advisor/debt-relief/debt-avalanche-method-how-it-works/.

Emmons, R. A. 2003. "Personal Goals, Life Meaning, and Virtue: Wellsprings of a positive Life." *American Psychological a* 105-128.

Farrar, Steven. 2022. *Point Man*. Colorado Springs, CO: Multnomah.

Fooducate. n.d. *Fooducate*. Accessed January 18, 2025. https://www.fooducate.com/.

Headspace. n.d. *Headspace.com*. Accessed August 19, 2024. https://www.headspace.com/.

Kagan, Julia. 2024. *Zero-Based Budgeting: What it is and How to Use It.* June 8. Accessed December 18, 2024. https://www.investopedia.com/terms/z/zbb.asp.

Kamel, George. 2024. *How the Debt Snowball Method Works.* August 14. Accessed December 18, 2024. https://www.ramseysolutions.com/debt/how-the-debt-snowball-method-works.

Kendrick, Alex and Kendrick, Stephen. 2013. *The Love Dare.* Nashville, TN: B&H Books.

Lake, Rebecca. 2025. *How to Use the Envelope Budgeting System.* January 23. Accessed February 5, 2025. https://www.investopedia.com/envelope-budgeting-system-5208026.

LoseIt! n.d. *Loseit.com.* Accessed January 18, 2025. https://www.loseit.com/.

Maxwell, John C. 2007. *The Maxwell Leadership Bible.* Nashville, TN: Thomas Nelson .

myfitnesspal. n.d. *myfitnesspal.com.* Accessed January 15, 2025. https://www.myfitnesspal.com/.

Shirer, Priscilla. 2015. *The Armor of God.* Nashville, TN: Lifeway Press.

Stapleton, Bruce. 2011. "Lifegevity Wellness Program." *BruceStapleton.com.* March 15. Accessed January 8, 2025. https://brucestapleton.com/lifegevity-wellness/.

Stapleton, Bruce. 2001. *Lifegevity Wellness Program.* White paper, Dayton, OH: Elan Vital, Inc. .

Stapleton, Bruce. 2009. *Stress Management - A Guaranteed Approach for Maximizing Your Health.* E-report, Dayton, OH: Lifegevity Institute.

Traugott, John. 2014. "Achieving Your Goals: An Evidence-based Approach." *Michigan State University Extension.* August 26. Accessed January 5, 2025. https://www.canr.msu.edu/news/achieving_your_goals_an_evidence_based_approach.

Whiteside, Eric. 2024. *The 50/30/20 Budget Rule Explained with Examples.* August 22. Accessed December 12, 2024. https://www.investopedia.com/ask/answers/022916/what-502030-budget-rule.asp.

Williams, Eli. 2016. *Father Love - The Powerful Resource Every Child Needs.* Springfield, OH: Xulon Press.

All Scripture quotations and references, unless otherwise indicated, are taken from YouVersion Bible app at Bible.com from the (NIV) New International Version Bible.

Printed in the United States
by Baker & Taylor Publisher Services